TOTAL HERMETICISM PHILOSOPHY COLLECTION

The Kybalion, Hermetica and The Secret Teachings of All Ages

HERMES TRISMEGISTUS   THREE INITIATES
WALTER SCOTT   MANLY P. HALL

Foreword by NOAH MARKS

Translated by THE YOGUI PUBLICATION SOCIETY

Translated by WALTER SCOTT

CONTENTS

Introduction   v
Historical Context   xi

THE KYBALION

1. THE HERMETIC PHILOSOPHY   3
2. THE SEVEN HERMETIC PRINCIPLES   9
3. MENTAL TRANSMUTATION   19
4. THE ALL   24
5. THE MENTAL UNIVERSE   31
6. THE DIVINE PARADOX   38
7. "THE ALL" IN ALL   48
8. PLANES OF CORRESPONDENCE   57
9. VIBRATION   70
10. POLARITY   77
11. RHYTHM   83
12. CAUSATION   90
13. GENDER   97
14. MENTAL GENDER   103
    Annotations and Thoughts of The Kybalion   114
15. HERMETIC AXIOMS   125

THE CORPUS HERMETICUM

1. Poemandres, the Shepherd of Men   135
2. To Asclepius   147
3. The Sacred Sermon   155
4. The Cup or Monad   158
5. Though Unmanifest God Is Most Manifest   164
6. In God Alone Is Good And Elsewhere Nowhere   170
7. The Greatest Ill Among Men is Ignorance of God   175

8. That No One of Existing Things doth Perish, but Men in Error Speak of Their Changes as Destructions and as Deaths	177
9. On Thought and Sense	180
10. The Key	186
11. Mind Unto Hermes	199
12. About The Common Mind	210
13. The Secret Sermon on the Mountain	221

THE LIFE AND TEACHINGS OF THOTH HERMES TRISMEGISTUS

Introduction	235
1. SUPPOSITIONS CONCERNING THE IDENTITY OF HERMES	237
2. THE MUTILATED HERMETIC FRAGMENTS	239
3. THE BOOK OF THOTH	243
4. POIMANDRES, THE VISION OF HERMES	245

INTRODUCTION

We take great pleasure in presenting to the attention of students and investigators of the Secret Doctrines this little work based upon the world-old Hermetic Teachings. There has been so little written upon this subject, not withstanding the countless references to the Teachings in the many works upon occultism, that the many earnest searchers after the Arcane Truths will doubtless welcome the appearance of this present volume.

The purpose of this work is not the enunciation of any special philosophy or doctrine, but rather is to give to the students a statement of the Truth that will serve to reconcile the many bits of occult knowledge that they may have acquired, but which are apparently opposed to each other and which often serve to discourage and disgust the beginner in the study. Our intent is not to erect a new Temple of Knowledge, but rather to place in the hands of the student a Master-Key with which he may open the many inner doors in the Temple of Mystery through the main portals he has already entered.

There is no portion of the occult teachings possessed by the world which have been so closely guarded as the fragments of the Hermetic Teachings which have come down to us over the tens of centuries which have elapsed since the lifetime of its great founder, Hermes Trismegistus, the "scribe of the gods," who dwelt in old Egypt in the days when the present race of men was in its infancy. Contemporary with Abraham, and, if the legends be true, an instructor of that venerable sage, Hermes was, and is, the Great Central Sun of Occultism, whose rays have served to illumine the countless teachings which have been promulgated since his time. All the fundamental and basic teachings embedded in the esoteric teachings of every race may be traced back to Hermes. Even the most ancient teachings of India undoubtedly have their roots in the original Hermetic Teachings.

From the land of the Ganges many advanced occultists wandered to the land of Egypt, and sat at the feet of the Master. From him they obtained the Master-Key which explained and reconciled their divergent views, and thus the Secret Doctrine was firmly established. From other lands also came the learned ones, all of whom regarded Hermes as the Master of Masters, and his influence was so great that in spite of the many wanderings from the path on the part of the centuries of teachers in these different lands, there may still be found a certain basic resemblance and correspondence which underlies the many and often quite divergent theories entertained and taught by the occultists of these different lands today. The student of Comparative Religions will be able to perceive the influence of the Hermetic Teachings in every religion worthy of the name, now known to man, whether it be a dead religion or one in full vigor in our own times. There is always certain correspondence in spite of the contradictory features, and the Hermetic Teachings act as the Great Reconciler.

The lifework of Hermes seems to have been in the direction of planting the great Seed-Truth which has grown and blossomed in so many strange forms, rather than to establish a school of philosophy which would dominate, the world's thought. But, nevertheless, the original truths taught by him have been kept intact in their original purity by a few men each age, who, refusing great numbers of half-developed students and followers, followed the Hermetic custom and reserved their truth for the few who were ready to comprehend and master it. From lip to ear the truth has been handed down among the few. There have always been a few Initiates in each generation, in the various lands of the earth, who kept alive the sacred flame of the Hermetic Teachings, and such have always been willing to use their lamps to re-light the lesser lamps of the outside world, when the light of truth grew dim, and clouded by reason of neglect, and when the wicks became clogged with foreign matter. There were always a few to tend faithfully the altar of the Truth, upon which was kept alight the Perpetual Lamp of Wisdom. These men devoted their lives to the labor of love which the poet has so well stated in his lines:

"O, let not the flame die out! Cherished age after age in its dark cavern—in its holy temples cherished. Fed by pure ministers of love—let not the flame die out!"

These men have never sought popular approval, nor numbers of followers. They are indifferent to these things, for they know how few there are in each generation who are ready for the truth, or who would recognize it if it were presented to them. They reserve the "strong meat for men," while others furnish the "milk for babes." They reserve their pearls of wisdom for the few elect, who recognize their value and who wear them in their crowns, instead of casting them before the materialistic vulgar swine, who would trample them in the mud and mix them with their disgusting mental food. But still these men have never forgotten or overlooked the original teachings of Hermes, regarding the passing on of the words of truth to those ready to receive it, which teaching is stated in The Kybalion as follows: "Where fall the footsteps of the Master, the ears of those ready for his Teaching open wide." And again: "When the ears of the student are ready to hear, then cometh the lips to fill them with wisdom." But their customary attitude has always been strictly in accordance with the other Hermetic aphorism, also in The Kybalion: "The lips of Wisdom are closed, except to the ears of Understanding."

There are those who have criticized this attitude of the Hermetists, and who have claimed that they did not manifest the proper spirit in their policy of seclusion and reticence. But a moment's glance back over the pages of history will show the wisdom of the Masters, who knew the folly of attempting to teach to the world that which it was neither ready or willing to receive. The Hermetists have never sought to be martyrs, and have, instead, sat silently aside with a pitying smile on their closed lips, while the "heathen raged noisily about them" in their customary amusement of putting to death and torture the honest but misguided enthusiasts who imagined that they could force upon a race of barbarians the truth capable of being understood only by the elect who had advanced along The Path.

And the spirit of persecution has not as yet died out in the land. There are certain Hermetic Teachings, which, if publicly promulgated, would bring down upon the teachers a great cry of scorn and revilement from the multitude, who would again raise the cry of "Crucify! Crucify."

In this little work we have endeavored to give you an idea of the fundamental teachings of The Kybalion, striving to give you the working Principles, leaving you to apply therm yourselves, rather than attempting to work out the teaching in detail. If you are a true student, you will be able to work out and apply these Principles—if not, then you must develop yourself into one, for otherwise the Hermetic Teachings will be as "words, words, words" to you.

THE THREE INITIATES.

HISTORICAL CONTEXT

Since its foundation, religion has both stood the test of time and evolved with different periods it endured. From philosophy to science, most religions have blended well with different disciplines to align with various philosophies that have existed for centuries and can still be practiced today. One of these philosophies is Hermeticism. This work closely examines the broad subject of hermeticism, with a close look at its historical background.

Historical Background

Hermeticism refers to the philosophical system that relies on the teachings of Hermes Trismegistus. These teachings are composed of a hybrid mixture of beliefs and teachings relating to Hermes, a Greek god, and Thoth, an Egyptian god. Although Egypt had a lot of Occult origins and masters, one of the great masters was Hermes Trismegistus. Hermes was considered the father of Occult wisdom because he possessed unparalleled knowledge of astrology. He was regarded as a contemporary of

Christian Abraham. After living for almost three hundred years, he passed from the physical world, and Egyptians deified him as the "the god of Wisdom".

One of the characteristics of hermetic philosophy was secrecy. This characteristic was so common that even today, Hermetic teachings, available in every country and religion, cannot be related to any specific origin or country.

Philosophy

One of the evident features of Hermeticism is that it is composed of a mixture of ancient Greece and Egyptian philosophies. This philosophy can be broken down into seven basic principles found in the most poignant and crucial Hermetic source.

One of the great teachings in the Kybalion is the principle of mentalism which summarizes that everything, in reality, is in mind. According to this teaching, everything, 'the all,' is an unknowable and undefinable spirit that exists in an infinite, living mind. In other words, the teaching argues that the world is a mental creation that results from the nature of "Energy," "Power," and "Matter," which work together with the mind to create "The All". In *Corpus Heremeticum,* Trismegisto argues that "the all" is an *aeon* or God. This means that reality is God, and God is within the mind of the cosmos. The nature of "the all" as the occupant of the mind can be found in the teachings of Thoth, who, upon meeting a dragon, asks a question about the mind. The response he gets is, "Take heed what you say, for *I am the Mind*--the Eternal Teacher. I am the Father of the Word--the Redeemer of all men--, and in the nature of the wise, the Word takes flesh" . From this response, the mind is occupied by the spirit *Thoth* who guides it to make decisions. That explains the origin of the word "thought."

Similarly, the teachings include the principle of correspondence, which argues that "there is always a correspondence between the laws and phenomena of various planes of Beings and Life". The ancient Egyptians used this principle to pry upon obstacles they could not see with bare eyes.

The principle of Vibration is also common teaching in hermeticism. According to this principle, everything is in motion because of vibration. However, the vibration frequencies of each of them are different because of the difference in the manifestation of matter, energy, and power. This knowledge enables individuals to control their vibrations to conquer natural phenomena.

Other principles in this teaching are the principle of polarity which states that everything exists as a dual or a pair of opposites. According to the teaching, "the thesis and antithesis are identical in nature, but different in degree" . The principle of rhythm also constitutes these teachings. It states that everything flows, rises, and falls. Hermetics says this principle applies to everything, including nature, humans, and animals. However, hermetics have learned to apply the Mental Law of Neutralization "scape its e acts upon themselves to a certain degree depending upon the Mastery of the Principle" .

The last two teachings are the principle of cause and effect and the principle of gender. According to hermetics, the principle of cause and effect states that every effect has its cause because "everything happens according to Law" . Although the cause and effect emanate from higher and lower planes, nothing can escape this principle. Hermetics have learned to rise above the cause and, sometimes, become the cause. They have achieved this by dominating their desires, mood, qualities of power, and character. The principle of gender teaches that everything has its masculine and feminine nature. In other words, it teaches that gender can be found in all planes. Therefore, "every male thing has a female element. Understanding this principle is essential in understanding the philosophy of mental and spiritual creation, hence exists as a gateway to understanding the mysteries of life.

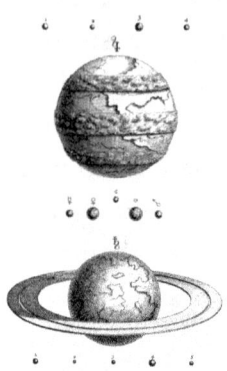

Conclusion

Hermeticism originates from the ancient world. Although it has remained under the rudder of the mainstream philosophy in the contemporary world, it controls most of the philosophical principles still applicable in modern times. Its teachings, centered around the teachings of Hermes and Thoth, are highly crucial in understanding the mind, the matter, and the energy that controls the cosmos.

THE KYBALION

I

THE HERMETIC PHILOSOPHY

"The lips of wisdom are closed, except to the ears of Understanding"

— THE KYBALION.

From old Egypt have come the fundamental esoteric and occult teachings which have so strongly influenced the philosophies of all races, nations and peoples, for several thousand years. Egypt, the home of the Pyramids and the Sphinx, was the birthplace of the Hidden Wisdom and Mystic Teachings. From her Secret Doctrine all nations have borrowed. India, Persia, Chaldea, Medea, China, Japan, Assyria, ancient Greece and Rome, and other ancient countries partook liberally at the feast of knowledge which the Hierophants and Masters of the Land of Isis so freely provided for those who came prepared to partake of the great store of Mystic and Occult Lore which the masterminds of that ancient land had gathered together.

In ancient Egypt dwelt the great Adepts and Masters who have never been surpassed, and who seldom have been equaled, during the centuries that have taken their processional flight since the days of the Great Hermes. In Egypt was located the Great Lodge of Lodges of the Mystics. At the doors of her Temples entered the Neophytes who afterward, as Hierophants, Adepts, and Masters, traveled to the four corners of the earth, carrying with them the precious knowledge which they were ready, anxious, and willing to pass on to those who were ready to receive the same. All students of the Occult recognize the debt that they owe to these venerable Masters of that ancient land.

But among these great Masters of Ancient Egypt there once dwelt one of whom Masters hailed as "The Master of Masters." This man, if "man" indeed he was, dwelt in Egypt in the earliest days. He was known as Hermes Trismegistus. He was the father of the Occult Wisdom; the founder of Astrology; the discoverer of Alchemy. The details of his life story are lost to history, owing to the lapse of the years, though several of the ancient countries disputed with each other in their claims to the honor of having furnished his birthplace—and this thousands of years ago. The date of his sojourn in Egypt, in that his last incarnation on this planet, is not now known, but it has been fixed at the early days of the oldest dynasties of Egypt—long before the days of Moses. The best authorities regard him as a contemporary of Abraham, and some of the Jewish traditions go so far as to claim that Abraham acquired a portion of his mystic knowledge from Hermes himself.

As the years rolled by after his passing from this plane of life (tradition recording that he lived three hundred years in the flesh), the Egyptians deified Hermes, and made him one of their gods, under the name of Thoth. Years after, the people of Ancient Greece also made him one of their many gods—calling him "Hermes, the god of Wisdom." The Egyptians revered his memory for many centuries-yes, tens of centuries— calling him "the Scribe of the Gods," and bestowing upon him, distinctively, his ancient title, "Trismegistus," which means "the thrice-great"; "the great-great"; "the greatest-great"; etc. In all the ancient lands, the name of Hermes Trismegistus was revered, the name being synonymous with the "Fount of Wisdom."

Even to this day, we use the term "hermetic" in the sense of "secret"; "sealed so that nothing can escape"; etc., and this by reason of the fact that the followers of Hermes always observed the principle of secrecy in their teachings. They did not believe in "casting pearls before swine," but rather held to the teaching "milk for babes"; "meat for strong men," both of which maxims are familiar to readers of the Christian scriptures, but both of which had been used by the Egyptians for centuries before the Christian era.

And this policy of careful dissemination of the truth has always characterized the Hermetics, even unto the present day. The Hermetic Teachings are to be found in all lands, among all religions, but never identified with any particular country, nor with any particular religious sect. This because of the warning of the ancient teachers against allowing the Secret Doctrine to become crystallized into a creed. The wisdom of this caution is apparent to all students of history. The ancient occultism of India and Persia degenerated, and was largely lost, owing to the fact that the teachers became priests, and so mixed theology with the philosophy, the result being that the occultism of India and Persia has been gradually lost amidst the mass of religious superstition, cults, creeds and "gods." So it was with Ancient Greece and Rome. So it was with the Hermetic Teachings of the Gnostics and Early Christians, which were lost at the time of Constantine, whose iron hand smothered philosophy with the blanket of theology, losing to the Christian Church that which was its very essence and spirit, and causing it to grope throughout several centuries before it found the way back to its ancient faith, the indications apparent to all careful observers in this Twentieth Century being that the Church is now struggling to get back to its ancient mystic teachings.

But there were always a few faithful souls who kept alive the Flame, tending it carefully, and not allowing its light to become extinguished. And thanks to these staunch hearts, and fearless minds, we have the truth still with us. But it is not found in books, to any great extent. It has been passed along from Master to Student; from Initiate to Hierophant; from lip to ear. When it was written down at all, its meaning was veiled in terms of alchemy and astrology so that only those possessing the key could read it aright. This was made necessary in order to avoid the persecutions of the theologians of the Middle Ages, who fought the Secret Doctrine with fire and sword; stake, gibbet and cross. Even to this day there will be found but few reliable books on the Hermetic Philosophy, although there are countless references to it in many books written on various phases of Occultism. And yet, the Hermetic Philosophy is the only Master Key which will open all the doors of the Occult Teachings!

> *In the early days, there was a compilation of certain Basic Hermetic Doctrines, passed on from teacher to student, which was known as "THE KYBALION,"*

the exact significance and meaning of the term having been lost for several centuries. This teaching, however, is known to many to whom it has descended, from mouth to ear, on and on throughout the centuries. Its precepts have never been written down, or printed, so far as we know. It was merely a collection of maxims, axioms, and precepts, which were non-understandable to outsiders, but which were readily understood by students, after the axioms, maxims, and precepts had been explained and exemplified by the Hermetic Initiates to their Neophytes. These teachings really constituted the basic principles of "The Art of Hermetic Alchemy," which, contrary to the general belief, dealt in the mastery of Mental Forces, rather than Material Elements-the Transmutation of one kind of Mental Vibrations into others, instead of the changing of one kind of metal into another. The legends of the "Philosopher's Stone" which would turn base metal into Gold, was an allegory relating to Hermetic Philosophy, readily understood by all students of true Hermeticism.

In this little book, of which this is the First Lesson, we invite our students to examine into the Hermetic Teachings, as set forth in THE KYBALION, and as explained by ourselves, humble students of the Teachings, who, while bearing the title of Initiates, are still students at the feet of HERMES, the Master. We herein give you many of the maxims, axioms and precepts of THE KYBALION, accompanied by explanations and illustrations which we deem likely to render the teachings more easily comprehended by the modern student, particularly as the original text is purposely veiled in obscure terms.

The original maxims, axioms, and precepts of THE KYBALION are printed herein, in italics, the proper credit being given. Our own work is printed in the regular way, in the body of the work. We trust that the many students to whom we now offer this little work will derive as much benefit from the study of its pages as have the many who have gone on before, treading the same Path to Mastery throughout the centuries that have passed since the times of HERMES TRISMEGISTUS—

the Master of Masters—the Great-Great. In the words of "THE KYBALION":

> *"Where fall the footsteps of the Master, the ears of those ready for his Teaching open wide."*

> *"When the ears of the student are ready to hear, then cometh the lips to fill them with Wisdom."*

So that according to the Teachings, the passage of this book to those ready for the instruction will attract the attention of such as are prepared to receive the Teaching. And, likewise, when the pupil is ready to receive the truth, then will this little book come to him, or her. Such is The Law. The Hermetic Principle of Cause and Effect, in its aspect of The Law of Attraction, will bring lips and ear together—pupil and book in company. So mote it be!

2
THE SEVEN HERMETIC PRINCIPLES

"The Principles of Truth are Seven; he who knows these, understandingly, possesses the Magic Key before whose touch all the Doors of the Temple fly open."

— THE KYBALION.

The Seven Hermetic Principles, upon which the entire Hermetic Philosophy is based, are as follows:

- 1. The Principle of Mentalism.
- 2. The Principle of Correspondence.
- 3. The Principle of Vibration.
- 4. The Principle of Polarity.
- 5. The Principle of Rhythm.
- 6. The Principle of Cause and Effect.
- 7. The Principle of Gender.

These Seven Principles will be discussed and explained as we proceed with these lessons. A short explanation of each, however, may as well be given at this point.

1. The Principle of Mentalism

"THE ALL IS MIND; The Universe is Mental."

This Principle embodies the truth that "All is Mind." It explains that THE ALL (which is the Substantial Reality underlying all the outward manifestations and appearances which we know under the terms of "The Material Universe"; the "Phenomena of Life"; "Matter"; "Energy"; and, in short, all that is apparent to our material senses) is SPIRIT which in itself is UNKNOWABLE and UNDEFINABLE, but which may be considered and thought of as AN UNIVERSAL, INFINITE, LIVING MIND.

It also explains that all the phenomenal world or universe is simply a Mental Creation of THE ALL, subject to the Laws of Created Things, and that the universe, as a whole, and in its parts or units, has its existence in the Mind of THE ALL, in which Mind we "live and move and have our being." This Principle, by establishing the Mental Nature of the Universe, easily explains all of the varied mental and psychic phenomena that occupy such a large portion of the public attention, and which, without such explanation, are non-understandable and defy scientific treatment. An understanding of this great Hermetic Principle of Mentalism enables the individual to readily grasp the laws of the Mental Universe, and to apply the same to his well-being and advancement. The Hermetic Student is enabled to apply intelligently the great Mental Laws, instead of using them in a haphazard manner. With the Master-Key in his possession, the student may unlock the many doors of the mental and psychic temple of knowledge, and enter the same freely and intelligently.

This Principle explains the true nature of "Energy," "Power," and "Matter," and why and how all these are subordinate to the Mastery of Mind. One of the old Hermetic Masters wrote, long ages ago: "He who grasps the truth of the Mental Nature of the Universe is well advanced on The Path to Mastery." And these words are as true today as at the time they were first written. Without this Master-Key, Mastery is impossible, and the student knocks in vain at the many doors of The Temple.

2. The Principle of Correspondence

"As above, so below; as below, so above."

THIS PRINCIPLE EMBODIES THE TRUTH THAT THERE IS ALWAYS a Correspondence between the laws and phenomena of the various planes of Being and Life. The old Hermetic axiom ran in these words: "As above, so below; as below, so above." And the grasping of this Principle gives one the means of solving many a dark paradox, and hidden secret of Nature. There are planes beyond our knowing, but when we apply the Principle of Correspondence to them we are able to understand much that would otherwise be unknowable to us. This Principle is of universal application and manifestation, on the various planes of the material, mental, and spiritual universe—it is an Universal Law. The ancient Hermetists considered this Principle as one of the most important mental instruments by which man was able to pry aside the obstacles which hid from view the Unknown. Its use even tore aside the Veil of Isis to the extent that a glimpse of the face of the goddess might be caught. Just as a knowledge of the Principles of Geometry enables man to measure distant suns and their movements, while seated in his observatory, so a knowledge of the Principle of Correspondence enables Man to reason intelligently from the Known to the Unknown. Studying the monad, he understands the archangel.

3. The Principle of Vibration

"Nothing rests; everything moves; everything vibrates."

THIS PRINCIPLE EMBODIES THE TRUTH THAT "EVERYTHING IS IN MOTION"; "everything vibrates"; "nothing is at rest"; facts which Modern Science endorses, and which each new scientific discovery tends to verify. And yet this Hermetic Principle was enunciated thousands of years ago, by the Masters of Ancient Egypt. This Principle explains that the differences between different manifestations of Matter, Energy, Mind, and even Spirit, result largely from varying rates of Vibration. From THE ALL, which is Pure Spirit, down to the grossest form of Matter, all is in vibration—the higher the vibration, the higher the position in the scale. The vibration of Spirit is at such an infinite rate of intensity and rapidity that it is practically at rest—just as a rapidly moving wheel seems to be motionless. And at the other end of the scale, there are gross forms of matter whose vibrations are so low as to seem at rest. Between these poles, there are millions upon millions of varying degrees of vibration. From corpuscle and electron, atom and molecule, to worlds and universes, everything is in vibratory motion. This is also true on the planes of energy and force (which are but varying degrees of vibration); and also on the mental planes (whose states depend upon vibrations); and even on to the spiritual planes. An understanding of this Principle, with the appropriate formulas, enables Hermetic students to control their own mental vibrations as well as those of others. The Masters also apply this Principle to the conquering of Natural phenomena, in various ways. "He who understands the Principle of Vibration, has grasped the scepter of power," says one of the old writers.

4. The Principle of Polarity

> *"Everything is Dual; everything has poles; everything has its pair of opposites; like and unlike are the same; opposites are identical in nature, but different in degree; extremes meet; all truths are but half-truths; all paradoxes may be reconciled."*

THIS PRINCIPLE EMBODIES THE TRUTH THAT "EVERYTHING IS dual"; "everything has two poles"; "everything has its pair of opposites," all of which were old Hermetic axioms. It explains the old paradoxes, that have perplexed so many, which have been stated as follows: "Thesis and antithesis are identical in nature, but different in degree"; "opposites are the same, differing only in degree"; "the pairs of opposites may be reconciled"; "extremes meet"; "everything is and isn't, at the same time"; "all truths are but half-truths"; "every truth is half-false"; "there are two sides to everything," etc., etc., etc. It explains that in everything there are two poles, or opposite aspects, and that "opposites" are really only the two extremes of the same thing, with many varying degrees between them. To illustrate: Heat and Cold, although "opposites," are really the same thing, the differences consisting merely of degrees of the same thing. Look at your thermometer and see if you can discover where "heat" terminates and "cold" begins! There is no such thing as "absolute heat" or "absolute cold"—the two terms "heat" and "cold" simply indicate varying degrees of the same thing, and that "same thing" which manifests as "heat" and "cold" is merely a form, variety, and rate of Vibration. So "heat" and "cold" are simply the "two poles" of that which we call "Heat"—and the phenomena attendant thereupon are manifestations of the Principle of Polarity. The same Principle manifests in the case of "Light and Darkness," which are the same thing, the difference consisting of varying degrees between the two poles of the phenomena. Where does "darkness" leave off, and "light" begin? What is the difference between "Large and Small"? Between "Hard and Soft"? Between "Black and White"? Between "Sharp and Dull"? Between "Noise and Quiet"? Between "High and Low"? Between "Positive and Negative"? The Principle of Polarity explains these paradoxes, and no other Principle can supersede it. The same Principle operates on the Mental Plane. Let us take a radical and extreme example—that of "Love and Hate," two mental states apparently totally different. And yet there are degrees of Hate and degrees of Love, and a middle point in which we use the terms "Like or Dislike," which shade into each other so gradually that sometimes we are at a loss to know whether we "like" or "dislike" or "neither." And all are simply degrees of the same thing, as you will see if you will but think a moment. And, more than this (and considered of more importance by the Hermetists), it is possible to change the vibrations of Hate to the vibrations of Love, in one's own mind, and in the minds of others. Many of you, who read these lines, have had personal experiences of the involuntary rapid transition from Love to Hate, and the reverse, in your own case and that of others. And you will therefore realize the possibility of this being accomplished by the use of the Will, by means of the Hermetic formulas. "Good and Evil" are but the poles of the same thing, and the Hermetist understands the art of transmuting Evil into Good, by means of an application of the Principle of Polarity. In short, the "Art of Polarization" becomes a phase of "Mental Alchemy" known and practiced by the ancient and modern Hermetic Masters. An understanding of the Principle will enable one to change his own Polarity, as well as that of others, if he will devote the time and study necessary to master the art.

5. The Principle of Rhythm

> *"Everything flows, out and in; everything has its tides; all things rise and fall; the pendulum-swing manifests in everything; the measure of the swing to the right is the measure of the swing to the left; rhythm compensates."*

THIS PRINCIPLE EMBODIES THE TRUTH THAT IN EVERYTHING there is manifested a measured motion, to and fro; a flow and inflow; a swing backward and forward; a pendulum-like movement; a tide-like ebb and flow; a high-tide and low-tide; between the two poles which exist in accordance with the Principle of Polarity described a moment ago. There is always an action and a reaction; an advance and a retreat; a rising and a sinking. This is in the affairs of the Universe, suns, worlds, men, animals, mind, energy, and matter. This law is manifest in the creation and destruction of worlds; in the rise and fall of nations; in the life of all things; and finally in the mental states of Man (and it is with this latter that the Hermetists find the understanding of the Principle most important). The Hermetists have grasped this Principle, finding its universal application, and have also discovered certain means to overcome its effects in themselves by the use of the appropriate formulas and methods. They apply the Mental Law of Neutralization. They cannot annul the Principle, or cause it to cease its operation, but they have learned how to escape its effects upon themselves to a certain degree depending upon the Mastery of the Principle. They have learned how to USE it, instead of being USED BY it. In this and similar methods, consist the Art of the Hermetists. The Master of Hermetics polarizes himself at the point at which he desires to rest, and then neutralizes the Rhythmic swing of the pendulum which would tend to carry him to the other pole. All individuals who have attained any degree of Self-Mastery do this to a certain degree, more or less unconsciously, but the Master does this consciously, and by the use of his Will, and attains a degree of Poise and Mental Firmness almost impossible of belief on the part of the masses who are swung backward and forward like a pendulum. This Principle and that of Polarity have been closely studied by the Hermetists, and the methods of counteracting, neutralizing, and USING them form an important part of the Hermetic Mental Alchemy.

6. The Principle of Cause and Effect

"Every Cause has its Effect; every Effect has its Cause; everything happens according to Law; Chance is but a name for Law not recognized; there are many planes of causation, but nothing escapes the Law."

THIS PRINCIPLE EMBODIES THE FACT THAT THERE IS A CAUSE for every Effect; an Effect from every Cause. It explains that: "Everything Happens according to Law"; that nothing ever "merely happens"; that there is no such thing as Chance; that while there are various planes of Cause and Effect, the higher dominating the lower planes, still nothing ever entirely escapes the Law. The Hermetists understand the art and methods of rising above the ordinary plane of Cause and Effect, to a certain degree, and by mentally rising to a higher plane they become Causers instead of Effects. The masses of people are carried along, obedient to environment; the wills and desires of others stronger than themselves; heredity; suggestion; and other outward causes moving them about like pawns on the Chessboard of Life. But the Masters, rising to the plane above, dominate their moods, characters, qualities, and powers, as well as the environment surrounding them, and become Movers instead of pawns. They help to PLAY THE GAME OF LIFE, instead of being played and moved about by other wills and environment. They USE the Principle instead of being its tools. The Masters obey the Causation of the higher planes, but they help to RULE on their own plane. In this statement there is condensed a wealth of Hermetic knowledge—let him read who can.

7. The Principle of Gender

"Gender is in everything; everything has its Masculine and Feminine Principles; Gender manifests on all planes."

THIS PRINCIPLE EMBODIES THE TRUTH THAT THERE IS GENDER manifested in everything—the Masculine and Feminine Principles ever at work. This is true not only of the Physical Plane, but of the Mental and even the Spiritual Planes. On the Physical Plane, the Principle manifests as SEX, on the higher planes it takes higher forms, but the Principle is ever the same. No creation, physical, mental or spiritual, is possible without this Principle. An understanding of its laws will throw light on many a subject that has perplexed the minds of men. The Principle of Gender works ever in the direction of generation, regeneration, and creation. Everything, and every person, contains the two Elements or Principles, or this great Principle, within it, him or her. Every Male thing has the Female Element also; every Female contains also the Male Principle. If you would understand the philosophy of Mental and Spiritual Creation, Generation, and Re-generation, you must understand and study this Hermetic Principle. It contains the solution of many mysteries of Life. We caution you that this Principle has no reference to the many base, pernicious and degrading lustful theories, teachings and practices, which are taught under fanciful titles, and which are a prostitution of the great natural principle of Gender. Such base revivals of the ancient infamous forms of Phallicism tend to ruin mind, body and soul, and the Hermetic Philosophy has ever sounded the warning note against these degraded teachings which tend toward lust, licentiousness, and perversion of Nature's principles. If you seek such teachings, you must go elsewhere for them—Hermeticism contains nothing for you along these lines. To the pure, all things are pure; to the base, all things are base.

3
MENTAL TRANSMUTATION

> *"Mind (as well as metals and elements) may be transmuted, from state to state; degree to degree; condition to condition; pole to pole; vibration to vibration. True Hermetic Transmutation is a Mental Art."*
>
> — THE KYBALION.

As we have stated, the Hermetists were the original alchemists, astrologers, and psychologists, Hermes having been the founder of these schools of thought. From astrology has grown modern astronomy; from alchemy has grown modern chemistry; from the mystic psychology has grown the modern psychology of the schools. But it must not be supposed that the ancients were ignorant of that which the modern schools suppose to be their exclusive and special property. The records engraved on the stones of Ancient Egypt show conclusively that the ancients had a full comprehensive knowledge of astronomy, the very building of the Pyramids showing the connection between their design and the study of astronomical science. Nor were they ignorant of

Chemistry, for the fragments of the ancient writings show that they were acquainted with the chemical properties of things; in fact, the ancient theories regarding physics are being slowly verified by the latest discoveries of modern science, notably those relating to the constitution of matter. Nor must it be supposed that they were ignorant of the so-called modern discoveries in psychology—on the contrary, the Egyptians were especially skilled in the science of Psychology, particularly in the branches that the modern schools ignore, but which, nevertheless, are being uncovered under the name of "psychic science" which is perplexing the psychologists of to-day, and making them reluctantly admit that "there may be something in it after all."

The truth is, that beneath the material chemistry, astronomy and psychology (that is, the psychology in its phase of "brain-action") the ancients possessed a knowledge of transcendental astronomy, called astrology; of transcendental chemistry, called alchemy; of transcendental psychology, called mystic psychology. They possessed the Inner Knowledge as well as the Outer Knowledge, the latter alone being possessed by modern scientists. Among the many secret branches of knowledge possessed by the Hermetists, was that known as Mental Transmutation, which forms the subject matter of this lesson.

"Transmutation" is a term usually employed to designate the ancient art of the transmutation of metals—particularly of the base metals into gold. The word "Transmute" means "to change from one nature, form, or substance, into another; to transform" (Webster). And accordingly, "Mental Transmutation" means the art of changing and transforming mental states, forms, and conditions, into others. So you may see that Mental Transmutation is the "Art of Mental Chemistry," if you like the term—a form of practical Mystic Psychology.

But this means far more than appears on the surface. Transmutation, Alchemy, or Chemistry on the Mental Plane is important enough in its effects, to be sure, and if the art stopped there it would still be one of the most important branches of study known to man. But this is only the beginning. Let us see why!

The first of the Seven Hermetic Principles is the Principle of Mentalism, the axiom of which is "THE ALL is Mind; the Universe is Mental," which means that the Underlying Reality of the Universe is Mind; and the Universe itself is Mental—that is, "existing in the Mind of THE ALL." We shall consider this Principle in succeeding lessons, but let us see the effect of the principle if it be assumed to be true.

If the Universe is Mental in its nature, then Mental Transmutation must be the art of CHANGING THE CONDITIONS OF THE UNIVERSE, along the lines of Matter, Force and mind. So you see, therefore, that Mental Transmutation is really the "Magic" of which the ancient; writers had so much to say in their mystical works, and about which they gave so few practical instructions. If All be Mental, then the art which enables one to transmute mental conditions must render the Master the controller of material conditions as well as those ordinarily called "mental."

As a matter of fact, none but advanced Mental Alchemists have been able to attain the degree of power necessary to control the grosser physical conditions, such as the control of the elements of Nature; the production or cessation of tempests; the production and cessation of earthquakes and other great physical phenomena. But that such men have existed, and do exist today, is a matter of earnest belief to all advanced occultists of all schools. That the Masters exist, and have these powers, the best teachers assure their students, having had experiences which justify them in such belief and statements. These Masters do not make public exhibitions of their powers, but seek seclusion from the crowds of men, in order to better work their may along the Path of Attainment. We mention their existence, at this point, merely to call your attention to the fact that their power is entirely Mental, and operates along the lines of the higher Mental Transmutation, under the Hermetic Principle of Mentalism.

> *"The Universe is Mental".*
>
> — THE KYBALION.

But students and Hermetists of lesser degree than Masters—the Initiates and Teachers—are able to freely work along the Mental Plane, in Mental Transmutation. In fact all that we call "psychic phenomena,"; "mental influence"; "mental science"; "new-thought phenomena," etc., operates along the same general lines, for there is but one principle involved, no matter by what name the phenomena be called.

The student and practitioner of Mental Transmutation works among the Mental Plane, transmuting mental conditions, states, etc., into others, according to various formulas, more or less efficacious. The various "treatments," "affirmations," "denials" etc., of the schools of mental science are but formulas, often quite imperfect and unscientific, of The Hermetic Art. The majority of modern practitioners are quite ignorant compared to the ancient masters, for they lack the fundamental knowledge upon which the work is based.

Not only may the mental states, etc., of one's self be changed or transmuted by Hermetic Methods; but also the states of others may be, and are, constantly transmuted in the same way, usually unconsciously, but often consciously by some understanding the laws and principles, in cases where the people affected are not informed of the principles of self-protection. And more than this, as many students and practitioners of modern mental science know, every material condition depending upon the minds of other people may be changed or transmuted in accordance with the earnest desire, will, and "treatments" of person desiring changed conditions of life. The public are so generally informed regarding these things at present, that we do not deem it necessary to mention the same at length, our purpose at this point being merely to show the Hermetic Principle and Art underlying all of these various forms of practice, good and evil, for the force can be used in opposite directions according to the Hermetic Principles of Polarity.

In this little book we shall state the basic principles of Mental Transmutation, that all who read may grasp the Underlying Principles, and thus possess the Master-Key that will unlock the many doors of the Principle of Polarity.

We shall now proceed to a consideration of the first of the Hermetic Seven Principles—the Principle of Mentalism, in which is explained the truth that "THE ALL is Mind; the Universe is Mental," in the words of The Kybalion. We ask the close attention, and careful study of this great Principle, on the part of our students, for it is really the Basic Principle of the whole Hermetic Philosophy, and of the Hermetic Art of Mental Transmutation.

4
THE ALL

> *"Under, and back of, the Universe of Time, Space and Change, is ever to be found The Substantial Reality—the Fundamental Truth."*
>
> — THE KYBALION.

"Substance" means: "that which underlies all outward manifestations; the essence; the essential reality; the thing in itself," etc. "Substantial" means: "actually existing; being the essential element; being real," etc. "Reality" means: "the state of being real; true, enduring; valid; fixed; permanent; actual," etc.

Under and behind all outward appearances or manifestations, there must always be a Substantial Reality. This is the Law. Man considering the Universe, of which he is a unit, sees nothing but change in matter, forces, and mental states. He sees that nothing really IS, but that everything is BECOMING and CHANGING. Nothing stands still-everything is being born, growing, dying-the very instant a thing reaches its height, it begins to decline—the law of rhythm is in constant operation—there is no reality, enduring quality, fixity, or substantiality in anything—nothing is permanent but Change. He sees all things evolving from other things, and resolving into other things—constant action and reaction; inflow and outflow; building up and tearing down; creation and destruction; birth, growth and death. Nothing endures but Change. And if he be a thinking man, he realizes that all of these changing things must be but outward appearances or manifestations of some Underlying Power—some Substantial Reality.

All thinkers, in all lands and in all times, have assumed the necessity for postulating the existence of this Substantial Reality. All philosophies worthy of the name have been based upon this thought. Men have given to this Substantial Reality many names-some have called it by the term of Deity (under many titles). Others have called it "The Infinite and Eternal Energy" others have tried to call it "Matter"—but all have acknowledged its existence. It is self-evident it needs no argument.

In these lessons we have followed the example of some of the world's greatest thinkers, both ancient and modern—the Hermetic. Masters—and have called this Underlying Power—this Substantial Reality—by the Hermetic name of "THE ALL," which term we consider the most comprehensive of the many terms applied by Man to THAT which transcends names and terms.

We accept and teach the view of the great Hermetic thinkers of all times, as well as of those illumined souls who have reached higher planes of being, both of whom assert that the inner nature of THE ALL is UNKNOWABLE. This must be so, for naught by THE ALL itself can comprehend its own nature and being.

The Hermetists believe and teach that THE ALL, "in itself," is and must ever be UNKNOWABLE. They regard all the theories, guesses and speculations of the theologians and metaphysicians regarding the inner nature of THE ALL, as but the childish efforts of mortal minds to grasp the secret of the Infinite. Such efforts have always failed and will always fail, from the very nature of the task. One pursuing such inquiries travels around and around in the labyrinth of thought, until he is lost to all sane reasoning, action or conduct, and is utterly unfitted for the work of life. He is like the squirrel which frantically runs around and around the circling treadmill wheel of his cage, traveling ever and yet reaching nowhere—at the end a prisoner still, and standing just where he started.

And still more presumptuous are those who attempt to ascribe to THE ALL the personality, qualities, properties, characteristics and attributes of themselves, ascribing to THE ALL the human emotions, feelings, and characteristics, even down to the pettiest qualities of mankind, such as jealousy, susceptibility to flattery and praise, desire for offerings and worship, and all the other survivals from the days of the childhood of the race. Such ideas are not worthy of grown men and women, and are rapidly being discarded.

(At this point, it may be proper for me to state that we make a distinction between Religion and Theology—between Philosophy and Metaphysics. Religion, to us, means that intuitional realization of the existence of THE ALL, and one's relationship to it; while Theology means the attempts of men to ascribe personality, qualities, and characteristics to it; their theories regarding its affairs, will, desires, plans, and designs, and their assumption of the office of " middle-men" between THE ALL and the people. Philosophy, to us, means the inquiry after knowledge of things knowable and thinkable; while Metaphysics means the attempt to carry the inquiry over and beyond the boundaries and into regions unknowable and unthinkable, and with the same tendency as that of Theology. And consequently, both Religion and Philosophy mean to us things having roots in Reality, while Theology and Metaphysics seem like broken reeds, rooted in the quicksands of ignorance, and affording naught but the most insecure support for the mind or soul of Man. we do not insist upon our students accepting these definitions—we mention them merely to show our position. At any rate, you shall hear very little about Theology and Metaphysics in these lessons.)

But while the essential nature of THE ALL is Unknowable, there are certain truths connected with its existence which the human mind finds itself compelled to accept. And an examination of these reports form a proper subject of inquiry, particularly as they agree with the reports of the Illumined on higher planes. And to this inquiry we now invite you.

> *"THAT which is the Fundamental Truth—the Substantial Reality—is beyond true naming, but the Wise Men call it THE ALL."*
>
> *"In its Essence, THE ALL is UNKNOWABLE."*
>
> *"But, the report of Reason must be hospitably received, and treated with respect."*
>
> — THE KYBALION.

The human reason, whose reports we must accept so long as we think at all, informs us as follows regarding THE ALL, and that without attempting to remove the veil of the Unknowable:

1) THE ALL must be ALL that REALLY IS. There can be nothing existing outside of THE ALL, else THE ALL would not be THE ALL.

2) THE ALL must be INFINITE, for there is nothing else to define, confine, bound, limit; or restrict THE ALL. It must be Infinite in Time, or ETERNAL,—it must have always continuously existed, for there is nothing else to have ever created it, and something can never evolve from nothing, and if it had ever "not been," even for a moment, it would not "be" now,—it must continuously exist forever, for there is nothing to destroy it, and it can never "not-be," even for a moment, because something can never become nothing. It must be Infinite in Space—it must be Everywhere, for there is no place outside of THE ALL—it cannot be otherwise than continuous in Space, without break, cessation, separation, or interruption, for there is nothing to break, separate, or interrupt its continuity, and nothing with which to "fill in the gaps." It must be Infinite in Power, or Absolute, for there is nothing to limit, restrict, restrain, confine, disturb or condition it—it is subject to no other Power, for there is no other Power.

3) THE ALL must be IMMUTABLE, or not subject to change in its real nature, for there is nothing to work changes upon it nothing into which it could change, nor from which it could have changed. It cannot be added to nor subtracted from; increased nor diminished; nor become greater or lesser in any respect whatsoever. It must have always been, and must always remain, just what it is now—THE ALL—there has never been, is not now, and never will be, anything else into which it can change.

THE ALL being Infinite, Absolute, Eternal and Unchangeable it must follow that anything finite, changeable, fleeting, and conditioned cannot be THE ALL. And as there is Nothing outside of THE ALL, in Reality, then any and all such finite things must be as Nothing in Reality. Now do not become befogged, nor frightened—we are not trying to lead you into the Christian Science field under cover of Hermetic Philosophy. There is a Reconciliation of this apparently contradictory state of affairs. Be patient, we will reach it in time.

We see around us that which is called "Matter," which forms the physical foundation for all forms. Is THE ALL merely Matter? Not at all! Matter cannot manifest Life or Mind, and as Life and Mind are manifested in the Universe, THE ALL cannot be Matter, for nothing rises higher than its own source—nothing is ever manifested in an effect that is not in the cause—nothing is evolved as a consequent that is not involved as an antecedent. And then Modern Science informs us that there is really no such thing as Matter—that what we call Matter is merely "interrupted energy or force," that is, energy or force at a low rate of vibration. As a recent writer has said "Matter has melted into Mystery." Even Material Science has abandoned the theory of Matter, and now rests on the basis of "Energy."

Then is THE ALL mere Energy or Force? Not Energy or Force as the materialists use the terms, for their energy and force are blind, mechanical things, devoid of Life or Mind. Life and Mind can never evolve from blind Energy or Force, for the reason given a moment ago: "Nothing can rise higher than its source—nothing is evolved unless it is involved—nothing manifests in the effect, unless it is in the cause. " And so THE ALL cannot be mere Energy or Force, for, if it were, then there would be no such things as Life and Mind in existence, and we know better than that, for we are Alive and using Mind to consider this very question, and so are those who claim that Energy or Force is Everything.

What is there then higher than Matter or Energy that we know to be existent in the Universe? LIFE AND MIND! Life and Mind in all their varying degrees of unfoldment! "Then," you ask, "do you mean to tell us that THE ALL is LIFE and MIND?" Yes! and No! is our answer. If you mean Life and Mind as we poor petty mortals know them, we say No! THE ALL is not that! "But what kind of Life and Mind do you mean?" you ask.

The answer is "LIVING MIND," as far above that which mortals know by those words, as Life and Mind are higher than mechanical forces, or matter—INFINITE LIVING MIND as compared to finite "Life and Mind." We mean that which the illumined souls mean when they reverently pronounce the word: "SPIRIT!"

"THE ALL" is Infinite Living Mind—the Illumined call it SPIRIT!

5

THE MENTAL UNIVERSE

"The Universe is Mental—held in the Mind of THE ALL."

— THE KYBALION.

THE ALL is SPIRIT! But what is Spirit? This question cannot be answered, for the reason that its definition is practically that of THE ALL, which cannot be explained or defined. Spirit is simply a name that men give to the highest conception of Infinite Living Mind—it means "the Real Essence"—it means Living Mind, as much superior to Life and Mind as we know them, as the latter are superior to mechanical Energy and Matter. Spirit transcends our understanding, and we use the term merely that we may think or speak of THE ALL. For the purposes of thought and understanding, we are justified in thinking of Spirit as Infinite Living Mind, at the same time acknowledging that we cannot fully understand it. We must either do this or stop thinking of the matter at all.

Let us now proceed to a consideration of the nature of the Universe, as a whole and in its parts. What is the Universe? We have seen that there can be nothing outside of THE ALL. Then is the Universe THE ALL? No, this cannot be, because the Universe seems to be made up of MANY, and is constantly changing, and in other ways it does not measure up to the ideas that we are compelled to accept regarding THE ALL, as stated in our last lesson. Then if the Universe be not THE ALL, then it must be Nothing—such is the inevitable conclusion of the mind at first thought. But this will not satisfy the question, for we are sensible of the existence of the Universe. Then if the Universe is neither THE ALL, nor Nothing, what Can it be? Let us examine this question.

If the Universe exists at all, or seems to exist, it must proceed in some way from THE ALL—it must be a creation of THE ALL. But as something can never come from nothing, from what could THE ALL have created it. Some philosophers have answered this question by saying that THE ALL created the Universe from ITSELF—that is, from the being and substance of THE ALL. But this will not do, for THE ALL cannot be subtracted from, nor divided, as we have seen, and then again if this be so, would not each particle in the Universe be aware of its being THE ALL—THE ALL could not lose its knowledge of itself, nor actually BECOME an atom, or blind force, or lowly living thing. Some men, indeed, realizing that THE ALL is indeed ALL, and also recognizing that they, the men, existed, have jumped to the conclusion that they and THE ALL were identical, and they have filled the air with shouts of "I AM GOD," to the amusement of the multitude and the sorrow of sages. The claim of the corpuscle that: "I am Man!" would be modest in comparison.

But, what indeed is the Universe, if it be not THE ALL, not yet created by THE ALL having separated itself into fragments? What else can it be— of what else can it be made? This is the great question. Let us examine it carefully. We find here that the "Principle of Correspondence" (see Lesson I.) comes to our aid here. The old Hermetic axiom, "As above so below," may be pressed into service at this point. Let us endeavor to get a glimpse of the workings on higher planes by examining those on our own. The Principle of Correspondence must apply to this as well as to other problems.

Let us see! On his own plane of being, how does Man create? Well, first, he may create by making something out of outside materials. But this will not do, for there are no materials outside of THE ALL with which it may create. Well, then, secondly, Man pro-creates or reproduces his kind by the process of begetting, which is self-multiplication accomplished by transferring a portion of his substance to his offspring. But this will not do, because THE ALL cannot transfer or subtract a portion of itself, nor can it reproduce or multiply itself—in the first place there would be a taking away, and in the second case a multiplication or addition to THE ALL, both thoughts being an absurdity. Is there no third way in which MAN creates? Yes, there is—he CREATES MENTALLY! And in so doing he uses no outside materials, nor does he reproduce himself, and yet his Spirit pervades the Mental Creation.

Following the Principle of Correspondence, we are justified in considering that THE ALL creates the Universe MENTALLY, in a manner akin to the process whereby Man creates Mental Images. And, here is where the report of Reason tallies precisely with the report of the Illumined, as shown by their teachings and writings. Such are the teachings of the Wise Men. Such was the Teaching of Hermes.

THE ALL can create in no other way except mentally, without either using material (and there is none to use), or else reproducing itself (which is also impossible). There is no escape from this conclusion of the Reason, which, as we have said, agrees with the highest teachings of the Illumined. Just as you, student, may create a Universe of your own in your mentality, so does THE ALL create Universes in its own Mentality. But your Universe is the mental creation of a Finite Mind, whereas that of THE ALL is the creation of an Infinite. The two are similar in kind, but infinitely different in degree. We shall examine more closely into the process of creation and manifestation as we proceed. But this is the point to fix in your minds at this stage: THE UNIVERSE, AND ALL IT CONTAINS, IS A MENTAL CREATION OF THE ALL. Verily indeed, ALL IS MIND!

> *"THE ALL creates in its Infinite Mind countless Universes, which exist for aeons of Time—and yet, to THE ALL, the creation, development, decline and death of a million Universes is as the time of the twinkling of an eye."*
>
> *"The Infinite Mind of THE ALL is the womb of Universes."*
>
> — THE KYBALION.

The Principle of Gender (see Lesson I. and other lessons to follow) is manifested on all planes of life, material mental and spiritual. But, as we have said before, "Gender" does not mean "Sex" sex is merely a material manifestation of gender. "Gender" means "relating to generation or creation." And whenever anything is generated or created, on any plane, the Principle of

Gender must be manifested. And this is true even in the creation of Universes.

Now do not jump to the conclusion that we are teaching that there is a male and female God, or Creator. That idea is merely a distortion of the ancient teachings on the subject. The true teaching is that THE ALL, in itself, is above Gender, as it is above every other Law, including those of Time and Space. It is the Law, from which the Laws proceed, and it is not subject to them. But when THE ALL manifests on the plane of generation or creation, then it acts according to Law and Principle, for it is moving on a lower plane of Being. And consequently it manifests the Principle of Gender, in its Masculine and Feminine aspects, on the Mental Plane, of course.

This idea may seem startling to some of you who hear it for the first time, but you have all really passively accepted it in your everyday conceptions. You speak of the Fatherhood of God, and the Motherhood of Nature—of God, the Divine Father, and Nature the Universal Mother—and have thus instinctively acknowledged the Principle of Gender in the Universe. Is this not so?

But, the Hermetic teaching does not imply a real duality—THE ALL is ONE—the Two Aspects are merely aspects of manifestation. The teaching is that The Masculine Principle manifested by THE ALL stands, in a way, apart from the actual mental creation of the Universe. It projects its Will toward the Feminine Principle (which may be called "Nature") whereupon the latter begins the actual work of the evolution of the Universe, from simple "centers of activity" on to man, and then on and on still higher, all according to well-established and firmly enforced Laws of Nature. If you prefer the old figures of thought, you may think of the Masculine Principle as GOD, the Father, and of the

Feminine Principle as NATURE, the Universal Mother, from whose womb all things have been born. This is more than a mere poetic figure of speech—it is an idea of the actual process of the creation of the Universe. But always remember, that THE ALL is but One, and that in its Infinite Mind the Universe is generated, created and exists.

It may help you to get the proper idea, if you will apply the Law of Correspondence to yourself, and your own mind. You know that the part of You which you call "I," in a sense, stands apart and witnesses the creation of mental Images in your own mind. The part of your mind in which the mental generation is accomplished may be called the "Me" in distinction from the "I" which stands apart and witnesses and examines the thoughts, ideas and images of the "Me." "As above, so below," remember, and the phenomena of one plane may be employed to solve the riddles of higher or lower planes.

Is it any wonder that You, the child, feel that instinctive reverence for THE ALL, which feeling we call "religion"—that respect, and reverence for THE FATHER MIND? Is it any wonder that, when you consider the works and wonders of Nature, you are overcome with a mighty feeling which has its roots away down in your inmost being? It is the MOTHER MIND that you are pressing close up to, like a babe to the breast.

Do not make the mistake of supposing that the little world you see around you—the Earth, which is a mere grain of dust in the Universe—is the Universe itself. There are millions upon millions of such worlds, and greater. And there are millions of millions of such Universes in existence within the Infinite Mind of THE ALL. And even in our own little solar system there are regions and planes of life far higher than ours, and beings compared to which we earth-bound mortals are as the slimy life-forms that dwell on the ocean's bed when compared to Man. There are beings with powers and attributes higher than Man has ever dreamed of the gods' possessing. And yet these beings were once as you, and still lower—and you will be even as they, and still higher, in time, for such is the Destiny of Man as reported by the Illumined.

And Death is not real, even in the Relative sense—it is but Birth to a new life—and You shall go on, and on, and on, to higher and still higher planes of life, for aeons upon aeons of time. The Universe is your home, and you shall explore its farthest recesses before the end of Time. You are dwelling in the Infinite Mind of THE ALL, and your possibilities and opportunities are infinite, both in time and space. And at the end of the Grand Cycle of Aeons, when THE ALL shall draw back into itself all of its creations—you will go gladly for you will then be able to know the Whole Truth of being At One with THE ALL. Such is the report of the Illumined—those who have advanced well along The Path.

And, in the meantime, rest calm and serene—you are safe and protected by the Infinite Power of the FATHER-MOTHER MIND.

> *"Within the Father-Mother Mind, mortal children are at home."*
>
> *"There is not one who is Fatherless, nor Motherless in the Universe."*
>
> — THE KYBALION.

6

THE DIVINE PARADOX

"The half-wise, recognizing the comparative unreality of the Universe, imagine that they may defy its Laws—such are vain and presumptuous fools, and they are broken against the rocks and torn asunder by the elements by reason of their folly. The truly wise, knowing the nature of the Universe, use Law against laws; the higher against the lower; and by the Art of Alchemy transmute that which is undesirable into that which is worthy, and thus triumph. Mastery consists not in abnormal dreams, visions and fantastic imaginings or living, but in using the higher forces against the lower—escaping the pains of the lower planes by vibrating on the higher. Transmutation, not presumptuous denial, is the weapon of the Master."

— THE KYBALION.

This is the Paradox of the Universe, resulting from the Principle of Polarity which manifests when THE ALL begins to Create— hearken to it for it points the difference between half-wisdom and wisdom. While to THE INFINITE ALL, the Universe, its Laws, its Powers, its life, its Phenomena, are as things witnessed in the state of Meditation or Dream; yet to all that is Finite, the Universe must be treated as Real, and life, and action, and thought, must be based thereupon, accordingly, although with an ever understanding of the Higher Truth. Each according to its own Plane and Laws. Were THE ALL to imagine that the Universe were indeed Reality, then woe to the Universe, for there would be then no escape from lower to higher, divineward —then would the Universe become a fixity and progress would become impossible. And if Man, owing to half-wisdom, acts and lives and thinks of the Universe as merely a dream (akin to his own finite dreams) then indeed does it so become for him, and like a sleep-walker he stumbles ever around and around in a circle, making no progress, and being forced into an awakening at last by his falling bruised and bleeding over the Natural Laws which he ignored. Keep your mind ever on the Star, but let your eyes watch over your footsteps, lest you fall into the mire by reason of your upward gaze. Remember the Divine Paradox, that while the Universe IS NOT, still IT IS. Remember ever the Two Poles of Truth the Absolute and the Relative. Beware of Half-Truths.

What Hermetists know as "the Law of Paradox" is an aspect of the Principle of Polarity. The Hermetic writings are filled with references to the appearance of the Paradox in the consideration of the problems of Life and Being. The Teachers are constantly warning their students against the error of omitting the "other side" of any question. And their warnings are particularly directed to the problems of the Absolute and the Relative, which perplex all students of philosophy, and which cause so many to think and act contrary to what is generally known as "common sense." And we caution all students to be sure to grasp the Divine Paradox of the Absolute and Relative, lest they become entangled in the mire of the Half-Truth. With this in view this particular lesson has been written. Read it carefully!

The first thought that comes to the thinking man after he realizes the truth that the Universe is a Mental Creation of THE ALL, is that the Universe and all that it contains is a mere illusion; an unreality; against which idea his instincts revolt. But this, like all other great truths, must be considered both from the Absolute and the Relative points of view. From the Absolute viewpoint, of course, the Universe is in the nature of an illusion, a dream, a phantasmagoria, as compared to THE ALL in itself. We recognize this even in our ordinary view, for we speak of the world as "a fleeting show" that comes and goes, is born and dies —for the element of impermanence and change, finiteness and unsubstantiality, must ever be connected with the idea of a created Universe when it is contrasted with the idea of THE ALL, no matter what may be our beliefs concerning the nature of both. Philosopher, metaphysician, scientist and theologian all agree upon this idea, and the thought is found in all forms of philosophical thought and religious conceptions, as well as in the theories of the respective schools of metaphysics and theology.

So, the Hermetic Teachings do not preach the unsubstantiality of the Universe in any stronger terms than those more familiar to you, although their presentation of the subject may seem somewhat more startling. Anything that has a beginning and an ending must be, in a sense, unreal and untrue, and the Universe comes under the rule, in all schools of thought. From the Absolute point of view, there is nothing Real except THE ALL, no matter what terms we may use in thinking of, or discussing the subject. Whether the Universe be created of Matter, or whether it be a Mental Creation in the Mind of THE ALL—it is unsubstantial, non-enduring, a thing of time, space and change. We want you to realize this fact thoroughly, before you pass judgment on the Hermetic conception of the Mental nature of the Universe. Think over any and all of the other conceptions, and see whether this be not true of them.

But the Absolute point of view shows merely one side of the picture—the other side is the Relative one. Absolute Truth has been defined as "Things as the mind of God knows them," while Relative Truth is "Things as the highest reason of Man understands them." And so while to THE ALL the Universe must be unreal and illusionary, a mere dream or result of meditation,—nevertheless, to the finite minds forming a part of that Universe, and viewing it through mortal faculties, the Universe is very real indeed, and must be so considered. In recognizing the Absolute view, we must not make the mistake of ignoring or denying the facts and phenomena of the Universe as they present themselves to our mortal faculties—we are not THE ALL, remember.

To take familiar illustrations, we all recognize the fact that matter "exists" to our senses—we will fare badly if we do not. And yet, even our finite minds understand the scientific dictum that there is no such thing as Matter from a scientific point of view—that which we call Matter is held to be merely an aggregation of atoms, which atoms themselves are merely a grouping of units of force, called electrons or "ions," vibrating and in constant circular motion. We kick a stone and we feel the impact—it seems to be real, notwithstanding that we know it to be merely what we have stated above. But remember that our foot, which feels the impact by means of our brains, is likewise Matter, so constituted of electrons, and for that matter so are our brains. And, at the best, if it were not by reason of our Mind, we would not know the foot or stone at all.

Then again, the ideal of the artist or sculptor, which he is endeavoring to reproduce in stone or on canvas, seems very real to him. So do the characters in the mind of the author; or dramatist, which he seeks to express so that others may recognize them. And if this be true in the case of our finite minds, what must be the degree of Reality in the Mental Images created in the Mind of the Infinite? Oh, friends, to mortals this Universe of Mentality is very real indeed—it is the only one we can ever know, though we rise from plane to plane, higher and higher in it. To know it otherwise, but actual experience, we must be THE ALL itself. It is true that the higher we rise in the scale—the nearer to "the mind of the Father" we reach—the more apparent becomes the illusory nature of finite things, but not until THE ALL finally withdraws us into itself does the vision actually vanish.

So, we need not dwell upon the feature of illusion. Rather let us, recognizing the real nature of the Universe, seek to understand its mental laws, and endeavor to use them to the best effect in our upward progress through life, as we travel from plane to plane of being. The Laws of the Universe are none the less "Iron Laws" because of the mental nature. All, except THE ALL, are bound by them. What is IN THE INFINITE MIND OF THE ALL is REAL in a degree second only to that Reality itself which is vested in the nature of THE ALL.

So, do not feel insecure or afraid—we are all HELD FIRMLY IN THE INFINITE MIND OF THE ALL, and there is naught to hurt us or for us to fear. There is no Power outside of THE ALL to affect us. So we may rest calm and secure. There is a world of comfort and security in this realization when once attained. Then "calm and peaceful do we sleep, rocked in the Cradle of the Deep"—resting safely on the bosom of the Ocean of Infinite Mind, which is THE ALL. In THE ALL, indeed, do "we live and move and have our being."

Matter is none the less Matter to us, while we dwell on the plane of Matter, although we know it to be merely an aggregation of "electrons," or particles of Force, vibrating rapidly and gyrating around each other in the formations of atoms; the atoms in turn vibrating and gyrating, forming molecules, which latter in turn form larger masses of Matter. Nor does Matter become less Matter, when we follow the inquiry still further, and learn from the Hermetic Teachings, that the "Force" of which the electrons are but units is merely a manifestation of the Mind of THE ALL, and like all else in the Universe is purely Mental in its nature. While on the Plane of matter, we must recognize its phenomena— we may control Matter (as all Masters of higher or lesser degree do), but we do so by applying the higher forces. We commit a folly when we attempt to deny the existence of Matter in the relative aspect. We may deny its mastery over us—and rightly so—but we should not attempt to ignore it in its relative aspect, at least so long as we dwell upon its plane.

Nor do the Laws of Nature become less constant or effective, when we know them, likewise, to be merely mental creations. They are in full effect on the various planes. We overcome the lower laws, by applying still higher ones—and in this way only. But we cannot escape Law or rise above it entirely. Nothing but THE ALL can escape Law—and that because THE ALL is LAW itself, from which all Laws emerge. The most advanced Masters may acquire the powers usually attributed to the gods of men; and there are countless ranks of being, in the great hierarchy of life, whose being and power transcends even that of the highest Masters among men to a degree unthinkable by mortals, but even the highest Master, and the highest Being, must bow to the Law, and be as Nothing in the eye of THE ALL. So that if even these highest Beings, whose powers exceed even those attributed by men to their gods—if even these are bound by and are subservient to Law, then imagine the presumption of mortal man, of our race and grade, when he dares to consider the Laws of Nature as "unreal!" visionary and illusory, because he happens to be able to grasp the truth that the Laws are Mental in nature, and simply Mental Creations of THE ALL. Those Laws which THE ALL intends to be governing Laws are not to be defied or argued away. So long as the Universe endures, will they endure— for the Universe exists by virtue of these Laws which form its framework and which hold it together.

The Hermetic Principle of Mentalism, while explaining the true nature of the Universe upon the principle that all is Mental, does not change the scientific conceptions of the Universe, Life, or Evolution. In fact, science merely corroborates the Hermetic Teachings. The latter merely teaches that the nature of the Universe is "Mental," while modern science has taught that it is "Material"; or (of late) that it is "Energy" at the last analysis. The Hermetic Teachings have no fault to find with Herbert Spencer's basic principle which postulates the existence of an "Infinite and Eternal Energy, from which all things proceed." In fact, the Hermetics recognize in Spencer's philosophy the highest outside statement of the workings of the Natural Laws that have ever been promulgated, and they believe Spencer to have been a reincarnation of an ancient philosopher who dwelt in ancient Egypt thousands of years ago, and who later incarnated as Heraclitus, the Grecian philosopher who lived B. C. 500. And they regard his statement of the "Infinite and Eternal Energy" as directly in the line of the Hermetic Teachings, always with the addition of their own doctrine that his "Energy" is the Energy of the Mind of THE ALL. With the Master-Key of the Hermetic Philosophy, the student of Spencer will be able to unlock many doors of the inner philosophical conceptions of the great English philosopher, whose work shows the results of the preparation of his previous incarnations. His teachings regarding Evolution and Rhythm are in almost perfect agreement with the Hermetic Teachings regarding the Principle of Rhythm.

So, the student of Hermetics need not lay aside any of his cherished scientific views regarding the Universe. All he is asked to do is to grasp the underlying principle of "THE ALL is Mind; the Universe is Mental—held in the mind of THE ALL." He will find that the other six of the Seven Principles will "fit into" his scientific knowledge, and will serve to bring out obscure points and to throw light in dark corners. This is not to be wondered at, when we realize the influence of the Hermetic thought of the early philosophers of Greece, upon whose foundations of thought the theories of modern science largely rest. The acceptance of the First Hermetic Principle (Mentalism) is the only great point of difference between Modern Science and Hermetic students, and Science is gradually moving toward the Hermetic position in its groping in the dark for a way out of the Labyrinth into which it has wandered in its search for Reality.

The purpose of this lesson is to impress upon the minds of our students the fact that, to all intents and purposes, the Universe and its laws, and its phenomena, are just as REAL, so far as Man is concerned, as they would be under the hypotheses of Materialism or Energism. Under any hypothesis the Universe in its outer aspect is changing, ever-flowing, and transitory—and therefore devoid of substantiality and reality. But (note the other pole of the truth) under the same hypotheses, we are compelled to ACT AND LIVE as if the fleeting things were real and substantial. With this difference, always, between the various hypotheses—that under the old views Mental Power was ignored as a Natural Force, while under Mentalism it becomes the Greatest Natural Force. And this one difference revolutionizes Life, to those who understand the Principle and its resulting laws and practice.

So, finally, students all, grasp the advantage of Mentalism, and learn to know, use and apply the laws resulting therefrom. But do not yield to the temptation which, as The Kybalion states, overcomes the half-wise and which causes them to be hypnotized by the apparent unreality of things, the consequence being that they wander about like dream-people dwelling in a world of dreams, ignoring the practical work and life of man, the end being that "they are broken against the rocks and torn asunder by the elements, by reason of their folly." Rather follow the example of the wise, which the same authority states, "use Law against Laws; the higher against the lower; and by the Art of Alchemy transmute that which is undesirable into that which is worthy, and thus triumph." Following the authority, let us avoid the half-wisdom (which is folly) which ignores the truth that: "Mastery consists not in abnormal dreams, visions, and fantastic imaginings or living, but in using the higher forces against the lower—escaping the pains of the lower planes by vibrating on the higher." Remember always, student, that "Transmutation, not presumptuous denial, is the weapon of the Master." The above quotations are from The Kybalion, and are worthy of being committed to memory by the student.

We do not live in a world of dreams, but in an Universe which while relative, is real so far as our lives and actions are concerned. Our business in the Universe is not to deny its existence, but to LIVE, using the Laws to rise from lower to higher —living on, doing the best that we can under the circumstances arising each day, and living, so far as is possible, to our biggest ideas and ideals. The true Meaning of Life is not known to men on this plane .if, indeed, to any—but the highest authorities, and our own intuitions, teach us that we will make no mistake in living up to the best that is in us, so far as is possible, and realising the Universal tendency in the same direction in spite of apparent evidence to the contrary. We are all on The Path—and the road leads upward ever, with frequent resting places.

Read the message of The Kybalion—and follow the example of "the wise"—avoiding the mistake of "the half-wise" who perish by reason of their folly.

7
"THE ALL" IN ALL

"While All is in THE ALL, it is equally true that THE ALL is in ALL. To him who truly understands this truth hath come great knowledge."

— THE KYBALION.

How often have the majority of people heard repeated the statement that their Deity (called by many names) was "All in All" and how little have they suspected the inner occult truth concealed by these carelessly uttered words? The commonly used expression is a survival of the ancient Hermetic Maxim quoted above. As the Kybalion says: "To him who truly understands this truth, hath come great knowledge." And, this being so, let us seek this truth, the understanding of which means so much. In this statement of truth—this Hermetic Maxim—is concealed one of the greatest philosophical, scientific and religious truths.

We have given you the Hermetic Teaching regarding the Mental Nature of the Universe—the truth that "the Universe is Mental—held in the Mind of THE ALL." As the Kybalion says, in the passage quoted above: "All is in THE ALL." But note also the co-related statement, that: "It is equally true that THE ALL is in ALL." This apparently contradictory statement is reconcilable under the Law of Paradox. It is, moreover, an exact Hermetic statement of the relations existing between THE ALL and its Mental Universe. We have seen how "All is in THE ALL"—now let us examine the other aspect of the subject.

The Hermetic Teachings are to the effect that THE ALL is Imminent in ("remaining within; inherent; abiding within") its Universe, and in every part, particle, unit, or combination, within the Universe. This statement is usually illustrated by the Teachers by a reference to the Principle of Correspondence. The Teacher instructs the student to form a Mental Image of something, a person, an idea, something having a mental form, the favorite example being that of the author or dramatist forming an idea of his characters; or a painter or sculptor forming an image of an ideal that he wishes to express by his art. In each case, the student will find that while the image has its existence, and being, solely within his own mind, yet he, the student, author, dramatist, painter, or sculptor, is, in a sense, immanent in; remaining within; or abiding within, the mental image also. In other words, the entire virtue, life, spirit, of reality in the mental image is derived from the "immanent mind" of the thinker. Consider this for a moment, until the idea is grasped.

To take a modern example, let us say that Othello, Iago, Hamlet, Lear, Richard III, existed merely in the mind of Shakespeare, at the time of their conception or creation. And yet, Shakespeare also existed within each of these characters, giving them their vitality, spirit, and action. Whose is the "spirit" of the characters that we know as Micawber, Oliver Twist, Uriah Heep—is it Dickens, or have each of these characters a personal spirit, independent of their creator? Have the Venus of Medici, the Sistine Madonna, the Apollo Belvidere, spirits and reality of their own, or do they represent the spiritual and mental power of their creators? The Law of Paradox explains that both propositions are true, viewed from the proper viewpoints. Micawber is both Micawber, and yet Dickens. And, again, while Micawber may be said to be Dickens, yet Dickens is not identical with Micawber. Man, like Micawber, may exclaim: "The Spirit of my Creator is inherent within me— and yet I am not HE!" How different this from the shocking half-truth so vociferously announced by certain of the half-wise, who fill the air with their raucous cries of: "I am God!" Imagine poor Micawber, or the sneaky Uriah Heep, crying: "I Am Dickens"; or some of the lowly clods in one of Shakespeare's plays, eloquently announcing that: "I Am Shakespeare!" THE ALL is in the earthworm, and yet the earthworm is far from being THE ALL. And still the wonder remains, that though the earth-worm exists merely as a lowly thing, created and having its being solely within the Mind of THE ALL—yet THE ALL is immanent in the earthworm, and in the particles that go to make up the earth-worm. Can there be any greater mystery than this of "All in THE ALL; and THE ALL in All?"

The student will, of course, realize that the illustrations given above are necessarily imperfect and inadequate, for they represent the creation of mental images in finite minds, while the Universe is a creation of Infinite Mind—and the difference between the two poles separates them. And yet it is merely a matter of degree—the same Principle is in operation—the Principle of Correspondence manifests in each—"As above, so Below; as Below, so above."

And, in the degree that Man realizes the existence of the Indwelling Spirit immanent within his being, so will he rise in the spiritual scale of life. This is what spiritual development means—the recognition, realization, and manifestation of the Spirit within us. Try to remember this last definition—that of spiritual development. It contains the Truth of True Religion.

There are many planes of Being—many sub-planes of Life—many degrees of existence in the Universe. And all depend upon the advancement of beings in the scale, of which scale the lowest point is the grossest matter, the highest being separated only by the thinnest division from the SPIRIT of THE ALL. And, upward and onward along this Scale of Life, everything is moving. All are on the Path, whose end is THE ALL. All progress is a Returning Home. All is Upward and Onward, in spite of all seemingly contradictory appearances. Such is the message of the Illumined.

The Hermetic Teachings concerning the process of the Mental Creation of the Universe, are that at the beginning of the Creative Cycle, THE ALL, in its aspect of Being, projects its Will toward its aspect of "Becoming" and the process of creation begins. It is taught that the process consists of the lowering of Vibration until a very low degree of vibratory energy is reached, at which point the grossest possible form of Matter is manifested. This process is called the stage of Involution, in which THE ALL becomes "involved," or "wrapped up," in its creation. This process is believed by the Hermetists to have a Correspondence to the mental process of an artist, writer, or inventor, who becomes so wrapped up in his mental creation as to almost forget his own existence and who, for the time being, almost "lives in his creation," If instead of "wrapped" we use the word "rapt," perhaps we will give a better idea of what is meant.

This Involuntary stage of Creation is sometimes called the "Outpouring" of the Divine Energy, just as the Evolutionary state is called the "Indrawing." The extreme pole of the Creative process is considered to be the furthest removed from THE ALL, while the beginning of the Evolutionary stage is regarded as the beginning of the return swing of the pendulum of Rhythm—a "coming home" idea being held in all of the Hermetic Teachings.

The Teachings are that during the "Outpouring," the vibrations become lower and lower until finally the urge ceases, and the return swing begins. But there is this difference, that while in the "Outpouring" the creative forces manifest compactly and as a whole, yet from the beginning of the Evolutionary or "Indrawing" stage, there is manifested the Law of Individualization—that is, the tendency to separate into Units of Force, so that finally that which left THE ALL as unindividualized energy returns to its source as countless highly developed Units of Life, having risen higher and higher in the scale by means of Physical, Mental and Spiritual Evolution.

The ancient Hermetists use the word "Meditation" in describing the process of the mental creation of the Universe in the Mind of THE ALL, the word "Contemplation" also being frequently employed. But the idea intended seems to be that of the employment of the Divine Attention. "Attention" is a word derived from the Latin root, meaning "to reach out; to stretch out," and so the act of Attention is really a mental "reaching out; extension" of mental energy, so that the underlying idea is readily understood when we examine into the real meaning of "Attention."

The Hermetic Teachings regarding the process of Evolution are that, THE ALL, having meditated upon the beginning of the

Creation—having thus established the material foundations of the Universe—having thought it into existence—then gradually awakens or rouses from its Meditation and in so doing starts into manifestation the process of Evolution, on the material mental and spiritual planes, successively and in order. Thus the upward movement begins—and all begins to move Spiritward. Matter becomes less gross; the Units spring into being; the combinations begin to form; Life appears and manifests in higher and higher forms; and Mind becomes more and more in evidence—the vibrations constantly becoming higher. In short, the entire process of Evolution, in all of its phases, begins, and proceeds according to the established "Laws of the Indrawing" process. All of this occupies aeons upon aeons of Man's time, each aeon containing countless millions of years, but yet the Illumined inform us that the entire creation, including Involution and Evolution, of an Universe, is but "as the twinkle of the eye" to THE ALL. At the end of countless cycles of aeons of time, THE ALL withdraws its Attention—its Contemplation and Meditation—of the Universe, for the Great Work is finished—and All is withdrawn into THE ALL from which it emerged. But Mystery of Mysteries—the Spirit of each soul is not annihilated, but is infinitely expanded—the Created and the Creator are merged. Such is the report of the Illumined!

The above illustration of the "meditation," and subsequent "awakening from meditation," of THE ALL, is of course but an attempt of the teachers to describe the Infinite process by a finite example. And, yet: "As Below, so Above." The difference is merely in degree. And just as THE ALL arouses itself from the meditation upon the Universe, so does Man (in time) cease from manifesting upon the Material Plane, and withdraws himself more and more into the Indwelling Spirit, which is indeed "The Divine Ego."

There is one more matter of which we desire to speak in this lesson, and that comes very near to an invasion of the Metaphysical field of speculation, although our purpose is merely to show the futility of such speculation. We allude to the question which inevitably comes to the mind of all thinkers who have ventured to seek the Truth. The question is: "WHY does THE ALL create Universes" The question may be asked in different forms, but the above is the gist of the inquiry.

Men have striven hard to answer this question, but still there is no answer worthy of the name. Some have imagined that THE ALL had something to gain by it, but this is absurd, for what could THE ALL gain that it did not already possess? Others have sought the answer in the idea that THE ALL "wished something to love" and others that it created for pleasure, or amusement; or because it "was lonely" or to manifest its power; —all puerile explanations and ideas, belonging to the childish period of thought.

Others have sought to explain the mystery by assuming that THE ALL found itself "compelled" to create, by reason of its own "internal nature"—its "creative instinct." This idea is in advance of the others, but its weak point lies in the idea of THE ALL being "compelled" by anything, internal or external. If its "internal nature," or "creative instinct," compelled it to do anything, then the "internal nature" or "creative instinct" would be the Absolute, instead of THE ALL, and so accordingly that part of the proposition falls. And, yet, THE ALL does create and manifest, and seems to find some kind of satisfaction in so doing. And it is difficult to escape the conclusion that in some infinite degree it must have what would correspond to an "inner nature," or "creative instinct," in man, with correspondingly infinite Desire and Will. It could not act unless it Willed to Act; and it would not Will to Act, unless it Desired to Act and it would not Desire to Act unless it obtained some Satisfaction thereby. And all of these things would belong to an "Inner Nature," and might be postulated as existing according to the Law of Correspondence. But, still, we prefer to think of THE ALL as acting entirely FREE from any influence, internal as well as external. That is the problem which lies at the root of difficulty—and the difficulty that lies at the root of the problem.

Strictly speaking, there cannot be said to be any "Reason" whatsoever for THE ALL to act, for a "reason" implies a "cause," and THE ALL is above Cause and Effect, except when it Wills to become a Cause, at which time the Principle is set into motion. So, you see, the matter is Unthinkable, just as THE ALL is Unknowable. Just as we say THE ALL merely "IS"—so we are compelled to say that "THE ALL ACTS BECAUSE IT ACTS." At the last, THE ALL is All Reason in Itself; All Law in Itself; All Action in Itself—and it may be said, truthfully, that THE ALL is Its Own Reason; its own Law; its own Act—or still further, that THE ALL; Its Reason; Its Act; is Law; are ONE, all being names for the same thing. In the opinion of those who are giving you these present lessons, the answer is locked up in the INNER SELF of THE ALL, along with its Secret of Being. The Law of Correspondence, in our opinion, reaches only to that aspect of THE ALL, which may be spoken of as "The Aspect of BECOMING." Back of that Aspect is "The Aspect of BEING" in which all Laws are lost in LAW; all Principles merge into PRINCIPLE—and THE ALL; PRINCIPLE; and BEING; are IDENTICAL, ONE AND THE SAME. Therefore, Metaphysical speculation on this point is futile. We go into the matter here, merely to show that we recognize the question, and also the absurdity of the ordinary answers of metaphysics and theology.

In conclusion, it may be of interest to our students to learn that while some of the ancient, and modern, Hermetic Teachers have rather inclined in the direction of applying the Principle of Correspondence to the question, with the result of the "Inner Nature" conclusion,—still the legends have it that HERMES, the Great, when asked this question by his advanced students, answered them by PRESSING HIS LIPS TIGHTLY TOGETHER and saying not a word, indicating that there WAS NO ANSWER. But, then, he may have intended to apply the axiom of his philosophy, that: "The lips of Wisdom are closed, except to the ears of Understanding," believing that even his advanced students did not possess the Understanding which entitled them to the Teaching. At any rate, if Hermes possessed the Secret, he failed to impart it, and so far as the world is concerned THE LIPS OF HERMES ARE CLOSED regarding it. And where the Great Hermes hesitated to speak, what mortal may dare to teach?

But, remember, that whatever be the answer to this problem, if indeed there be an answer the truth remains that: "While All is in THE ALL, it is equally true that THE ALL is in All." The Teaching on this point is emphatic. And, we may add the concluding words of the quotation: "To him who truly understands this truth, hath come great knowledge."

8
PLANES OF CORRESPONDENCE

"As above, so below; as below, so above."

— THE KYBALION.

The great Second Hermetic Principle embodies the truth that there is a harmony, agreement, and correspondence between the several planes of Manifestation, Life and Being. This truth is a truth because all that is included in the Universe emanates from the same source, and the same laws, principles, and characteristics apply to each unit, or combination of units, of activity, as each manifests its own phenomena upon its own plane.

For the purpose of convenience of thought and study, the Hermetic Philosophy considers that the Universe may be divided into three great classes of phenomena, known as the Three Great Planes, namely:

- 1. The Great Physical Plane.
- 2. The Great Mental Plane.

- 3. The Great Spiritual Plane.

These divisions are more or less artificial and arbitrary, for the truth is that all of the three divisions are but ascending degrees of the great scale of Life, the lowest point of which is undifferentiated Matter, and the highest point that of Spirit. And, moreover, the different Planes shade into each other, so that no hard and fast division may be made between the higher phenomena of the Physical and the lower of the Mental; or between the higher of the Mental and the lower of the Physical.

In short, the Three Great Planes may be regarded as three great groups of degrees of Life Manifestation. While the purposes of this little book do not allow us to enter into an extended discussion of, or explanation of, the subject of these different planes, still we think it well to give a general description of the same at this point.

At the beginning we may as well consider the question so often asked by the neophyte, who desires to be informed regarding the meaning of the word "Plane", which term has been very freely used, and very poorly explained, in many recent works upon the subject of occultism. The question is generally about as follows: "Is a Plane a place having dimensions, or is it merely a condition or state?" We answer: "No, not a place, nor ordinary dimension of space; and yet more than a state or condition. It may be considered as a state or condition, and yet the state or condition is a degree of dimension, in a scale subject to measurement." Somewhat paradoxical, is it not? But let us examine the matter. A "dimension," you know, is "a measure in a straight line, relating to measure," etc. The ordinary dimensions of space are length, breadth, and height, or perhaps length, breadth, height, thickness or circumference. But there is another dimension of "created things" or "measure in a straight line," known to occultists, and to scientists as well, although the latter have not as yet applied the term "dimension" to it—and this new dimension, which, by the way, is the much speculated -about "Fourth Dimension," is the standard used in determining the degrees or "planes."

This Fourth Dimension may be called "The Dimension of Vibration" It is a fact well known to modern science, as well as to the Hermetists who have embodied the truth in their "Third Hermetic Principle," that "everything is in motion; everything vibrates; nothing is at rest." From the highest manifestation, to the lowest, everything and all things Vibrate. Not only do they vibrate at different rates of motion, but as in different directions and in a different manner. The degrees of the rate of vibrations constitute the degrees of measurement on the Scale of Vibrations—in other words the degrees of the Fourth Dimension. And these degrees form what occultists call "Planes" The higher the degree of rate of vibration, the higher the plane, and the higher the manifestation of Life occupying that plane. So that while a plane is not "a place," nor yet "a state or condition," yet it possesses qualities common to both. We shall have more to say regarding the subject of the scale of Vibrations in our next lessons, in which we shall consider the Hermetic Principle of Vibration.

You will kindly remember, however, that the Three Great Planes are not actual divisions of the phenomena of the Universe, but merely arbitrary terms used by the Hermetists in order to aid in the thought and study of the various degrees and Forms of universal activity and life. The atom of matter, the unit of force, the mind of man, and the being of the arch -angel are all but degrees in one scale, and all fundamentally the same, the difference between solely a matter of degree, and rate of vibration—

all are creations of THE ALL, and have their existence solely within the Infinite Mind of THE ALL.

The Hermetists sub-divide each of the Three Great Planes into Seven Minor Planes, and each of these latter are also sub-divided into seven sub-planes, all divisions being more or less arbitrary, shading into each other, and adopted merely for convenience of scientific study and thought.

The Great Physical Plane, and its Seven Minor Planes, is that division of the phenomena of the Universe which includes all that relates to physics, or material things, forces, and manifestations. It includes all forms of that which we call Matter, and all forms of that which we call Energy or Force. But you must remember that the Hermetic Philosophy does not recognize Matter as a thing in itself, or as having a separate existence even in the Mind of THE ALL. The Teachings are that Matter is but a form of Energy—.that is, Energy at a low rate of vibrations of a certain kind. And accordingly the Hermetists classify Matter under the head of Energy, and give to it three of the Seven Minor Planes of the Great Physical Plane.

THESE SEVEN MINOR PHYSICAL PLANES ARE AS FOLLOWS:

1. The Plane of Matter (A)

2. The Plane of Matter (B)

3. The Plane of Matter (C)

4. The Plane of Ethereal Substance

5. The Plane of Energy (A)

6. The Plane of Energy (B)

7. The Plane of Energy (C)

THE PLANE OF MATTER (A) COMPRISES THE FORMS OF MATTER in its form of solids, liquids, and gases, as generally recognized by the text-books on physics. The Plane of Matter (B) comprises certain higher and more subtle forms of Matter of the existence of which modern science is but now recognizing, the phenomena of Radiant Matter, in its phases of radium, etc., belonging to the lower sub-division of this Minor Plane. The Plane of Matter (C) comprises forms of the most subtle and tenuous Matter, the existence of which is not suspected by ordinary scientists. The Plane of Ethereal Substance comprises that which science speaks of as "The Ether", a substance of extreme tenuity and elasticity, pervading all Universal Space, and acting as a medium for the transmission of waves of energy, such as light, heat, electricity, etc. This Ethereal Substance forms a connecting link between Matter (so-called) and Energy, and partakes of the nature of each. The Hermetic Teachings, however, instruct that this plane has seven sub-divisions (as have all of the Minor Planes), and that in fact there are seven ethers, instead of but one.

Next above the Plane of Ethereal Substance comes the Plane of Energy (A), which comprises the ordinary forms of Energy known to science, its seven sub-planes being, respectively, Heat; Light; Magnetism; Electricity, and Attraction (including Gravitation, Cohesion, Chemical Affinity, etc.) and several other forms of energy indicated by scientific experiments but not as yet named or classified. The Plane of Energy (B) comprises seven subplanes of higher forms of energy not as yet discovered by science, but which have been called "Nature's Finer Forces" and which are called into operation in manifestations of certain forms of mental phenomena, and by which such phenomena becomes possible. The Plane of Energy (C) comprises seven sub-planes of energy so highly organized that it bears many of the characteristics of "life," but which is not recognized by the minds of men on the ordinary plane of development, being available for the use on beings of the Spiritual Plane alone—such energy is unthinkable to ordinary man, and may be considered almost as "the divine power." The beings employing the same are as "gods" compared even to the highest human types known to us.

The Great Mental Plane comprises those forms of "living things" known to us in ordinary life, as well as certain other forms not so well known except to the occultist. The classification of the Seven Minor Mental Planes is more or less satisfactory and arbitrary (unless accompanied by elaborate explanations which are foreign to the purpose of this particular work), but we may as well mention them. They are as follows:

- 1. The Plane of Mineral Mind
- 2. The Plane of Elemental Mind (A)
- 3. The Plane of Plant Mind
- 4. The Plane of Elemental Mind (B)
- 5. The Plane of Animal Mind
- 6. The Plane of Elemental Mind (C)
- 7. The Plane of Human Mind

The Plane of Mineral Mind comprises the "states or conditions" of the units or entities, or groups and combinations of the same, which animate the forms known to us as "minerals, chemicals, etc." These entities must not be confounded with the molecules, atoms and corpuscles themselves, the latter being merely the material bodies or forms of these entities, just as a man's body is but his material form and not "himself." These entities may be called "souls" in one sense, and are living beings of a low degree of development, life, and mind—just a little more than the units of "living energy" which comprise the higher sub-divisions of the highest Physical Plane. The average mind does not generally attribute the possession of mind, soul, or life, to the mineral kingdom, but all occultists recognize the existence of the same, and modern science is rapidly moving forward to the point-of-view of the Hermetic, in this respect. The molecules, atoms and corpuscles have their "loves and hates"; "likes and dislikes"; "attractions and repulsions". "affinities and non-affinities," etc., and some of the more daring of modern scientific minds have expressed the opinion that the desire and will, emotions and feelings, of the atoms differ only in degree from those of men. We have no time or space to argue this matter here. All occultists know it to be a fact, and others are referred to some of the more recent scientific works for outside corroboration. There are the usual seven sub-divisions to this plane.

The Plane of Elemental Mind (A) comprises the state or condition, and degree of mental and vital development of a class of entities unknown to the average man, but recognized to occultists. They are invisible to the ordinary senses of man, but, nevertheless, exist and play their part of the Drama of the Universe. Their degree of intelligence is between that of the mineral and chemical entities on the one hand, and of the entities of the plant kingdom on the other. There are seven subdivisions to this plane, also.

The Plane of Plant Mind, in its seven sub-divisions, comprises the states or conditions of the entities comprising the kingdoms of the Plant World, the vital and mental phenomena of which is fairly well understood by the average intelligent person, many new and interesting scientific works regarding "Mind and Life in

Plants" having been published during the last decade. Plants have life, mind and "souls," as well as have the animals, man, and super-man.

The Plane of Elemental Mind (B), in its seven sub-divisions, comprises the states and conditions of a higher form of "elemental" or unseen entities, playing their part in the general work of the Universe, the mind and life of which form a part of the scale between the Plane of Plant Mind and the Plane of Animal Mind, the entities partaking of the nature of both.

The Plane of Animal Mind, in its seven sub-divisions, comprises the states and conditions of the entities, beings, or souls, animating the animal forms of life, familiar to us all. It is not necessary to go into details regarding this kingdom or plane of life, for the animal world is as familiar to us as is our own.

The Plane of Elemental Mind (C), in its seven sub-divisions, comprises those entities or beings, invisible as are all such elemental forms, which partake of the nature of both animal and human life in a degree and in certain combinations. The highest forms are semi-human in intelligence.

The Plane of Human Mind, in its seven sub-divisions, comprises those manifestations of life and mentality which are common to Man, in his various grades, degrees, and divisions. In this connection, we wish to point out the fact that the average man of today occupies but the fourth sub-division of the Plane of Human Mind, and only the most intelligent have crossed the borders of the Fifth Sub-Division. It has taken the race millions of years to reach this stage, and it will take many more years for the race to move on to the sixth and seventh sub-divisions, and beyond. But, remember, that there have been races before us which have passed through these degrees, and then on to higher planes. Our own race is the fifth (with stragglers from the fourth) which has set foot upon The Path. And, then there are a few advanced souls of our own race who have outstripped the masses, and who have passed on to the sixth and seventh sub-division, and some few being still further on. The man of the Sixth Sub-Division will be "The Super-Man"; he of the Seventh will be "The Over-Man."

In our consideration of the Seven Minor Mental Planes, we have merely referred to the Three Elementary Planes in a general way. We do not wish to go into this subject in detail in this work, for it does not belong to this part of the general philosophy and teachings. But we may say this much, in order to give you a little clearer idea, of the relations of these planes to the more familiar ones—the Elementary Planes bear the same relation to the Planes of Mineral, Plant, Animal and Human Mentality and Life, that the black keys on the piano do to the white keys. The white keys are sufficient to produce music, but there are certain scales, melodies, and harmonies, in which the black keys play their part, and in which their presence is necessary. They are also necessary as "connecting links" of soul-condition; entity states, etc., between the several other planes, certain forms of development being attained therein—this last fact giving to the reader who can "read between the lines" a new light upon the processes of Evolution, and a new key to the secret door of the "leaps of life" between kingdom and kingdom. The great kingdoms of Elementals are fully recognized by all occultists, and the esoteric writings are full of mention of them. The readers of Bulwer's "Sanoni" and similar tales will recognize the entities inhabiting these planes of life.

Passing on from the Great Mental Plane to the Great Spiritual Plane, what shall we say? How can we explain these higher states of Being, Life and Mind, to minds as yet unable to grasp and understand the higher subdivisions of the Plane of Human

Mind? The task is impossible. We can speak only in the most general terms. How may Light be described to a man born blind—how sugar, to a man who has never tasted anything sweet—how harmony, to one born deaf?

All that we can say is that the Seven Minor Planes of the Great Spiritual Plane (each Minor Plane having its seven sub-divisions) comprise Beings possessing Life, Mind and Form as far above that of Man of to-day as the latter is above the earth-worm, mineral or even certain forms of Energy or Matter. The Life of these Beings so far transcends ours, that we cannot even think of the details of the same; their minds so far transcend ours, that to them we scarcely seem to "think," and our mental processes seem almost akin to material processes; the Matter of which their forms are composed is of the highest Planes of Matter, nay, some are even said to be "clothed in Pure Energy." What may be said of such Beings?

On the Seven Minor Planes of the Great Spiritual Plane exist Beings of whom we may speak as Angels; Archangels; Demi-Gods. On the lower Minor Planes dwell those great souls whom we call Masters and Adepts. Above them come the Great Hierarchies of the Angelic Hosts, unthinkable to man; and above those come those who may without irreverence be called "The Gods," so high in the scale of Being are they, their being, intelligence and power being akin to those attributed by the races of men to their conceptions of Deity. These Beings are beyond even the highest flights of the human imagination, the word "Divine" being the only one applicable to them. Many of these Beings, as well as the Angelic Host, take the greatest interest in the affairs of the Universe and play an important part in its affairs. These Unseen Divinities and Angelic Helpers extend their influence freely and powerfully, in the process of Evolution, and Cosmic Progress. Their occasional intervention and assistance in human affairs have led to the many legends, beliefs, religions and traditions of the race, past and present. They have superimposed their knowledge and power upon the world, again and again, all under the Law of THE ALL, of course.

But, yet, even the highest of these advanced Beings exist merely as creations of, and in, the Mind of THE ALL, and are subject to the Cosmic Processes and Universal Laws. They are still Mortal. We may call them "gods" if we like, but still they are but the Elder Brethren of the Race,—the advanced souls who have outstripped their brethren, and who have foregone the ecstasy of Absorption by THE ALL, in order to help the race on its upward journey along The Path. But, they belong to the Universe, and are subject to its conditions—they are mortal—and their plane is below that of Absolute Spirit.

Only the most advanced Hermetists are able to grasp the Inner Teachings regarding the state of existence, and the powers manifested on the Spiritual Planes. The phenomena is so much higher than that of the Mental Planes that a confusion of ideas would surely result from an attempt to describe the same. Only those whose minds have been carefully trained along the lines of the Hermetic Philosophy for years—yes, those who have brought with them from other incarnations the knowledge acquired previously—can comprehend just what is meant by the Teaching regarding these Spiritual Planes. And much of these Inner Teachings is held by the Hermetists as being too sacred, important and even dangerous for general public dissemination. The intelligent student may recognize what we mean by this when we state that the meaning of "Spirit" as used by the Hermetists is akin to "Living Power"; "Animated Force;" "Inner Essence;" "Essence of Life," etc., which meaning must not be confounded with that usually and commonly employed in connection with the term, i.e., "religious; ecclesiastical; spiritual;

ethereal; holy," etc., etc. To occultists the word "Spirit" is used in the sense of "The Animating Principle," carrying with it the idea of Power, Living Energy, Mystic Force, etc. And occultists know that that which is known to them as "Spiritual Power" may be employed for evil as well as good ends (in accordance with the Principle of Polarity), a fact which has been recognized by the majority of religions in their conceptions of Satan, Beelzebub, the Devil, Lucifer, Fallen Angels, etc. And so the knowledge regarding these Planes has been kept in the Holy of Holies in all Esoteric Fraternities and Occult Orders,—in the Secret Chamber of the Temple. But this may be said here, that those who have attained high spiritual powers and have misused them, have a terrible fate in store for them, and the swing of the pendulum of Rhythm will inevitably swing them back to the furthest extreme of Material existence, from which point they must retrace their steps Spiritward, along the weary rounds of The Path, but always with the added torture of having always with them a lingering memory of the heights from which they fell owing to their evil actions. The legends of the Fallen Angels have a basis in actual facts, as all advanced occultists know. The striving for selfish power on the Spiritual Planes inevitably results in the selfish soul losing its spiritual balance and falling back as far as it had previously risen. But to even such a soul, the opportunity of a return is given—and such souls make the return journey, paying the terrible penalty according to the invariable Law.

In conclusion we would again remind you that according to the Principle of Correspondence, which embodies the truth: "As Above so Below; as Below, so Above," all of the Seven Hermetic Principles are in full operation on all of the many planes, Physical Mental and Spiritual. The Principle of Mental Substance of course applies to all the planes, for all are held in the Mind of

THE ALL. The Principle of Correspondence manifests in all, for there is a correspondence, harmony and agreement between the several planes. The Principle of Vibration manifests on all planes, in fact the very differences that go to make the "planes" arise from Vibration, as we have explained. The Principle of Polarity manifests on each plane, the extremes of the Poles being apparently opposite and contradictory. The Principle of Rhythm manifests on each Plane, the movement of the phenomena having its ebb and flow, rise and flow, incoming and outgoing. The Principle of Cause and Effect manifests on each Plane, every Effect having its Cause and every Cause having its effect. The Principle of Gender manifests on each Plane, the Creative Energy being always manifest, and operating along the lines of its Masculine and Feminine Aspects.

"As Above so Below; as Below, so Above." This centuries old Hermetic axiom embodies one of the great Principles of Universal Phenomena. As we proceed with our consideration of the remaining Principles, we will see even more clearly the truth of the universal nature of this great Principle of Correspondence.

9
VIBRATION

"Nothing rests; everything moves; everything vibrates."

— THE KYBALION.

The great Third Hermetic Principle—the Principle of Vibration—embodies the truth that Motion is manifest in everything in the Universe—that nothing is at rest—that everything moves, vibrates, and circles. This Hermetic Principle was recognized by some of the early Greek philosophers who embodied it in their systems. But, then, for centuries it was lost sight of by the thinkers outside of the Hermetic ranks. But in the Nineteenth Century physical science re-discovered the truth and the Twentieth Century scientific discoveries have added additional proof of the correctness and truth of this centuries-old Hermetic doctrine.

The Hermetic Teachings are that not only is everything in constant movement and vibration, but that the "differences" between the various manifestations of the universal power are due entirely to the varying rate and mode of vibrations. Not only this, but that even THE ALL, in itself, manifests a constant vibration of such an infinite degree of intensity and rapid motion that it may be practically considered as at rest, the teachers directing the attention of the students to the fact that even on the physical plane a rapidly moving object (such as a revolving wheel) seems to be at rest. The Teachings are to the effect that Spirit is at one end of the Pole of Vibration, the other Pole being certain extremely gross forms of Matter. Between these two poles are millions upon millions of different rates and modes of vibration.

Modern Science has proven that all that we call Matter and Energy are but "modes of vibratory motion," and some of the more advanced scientists are rapidly moving toward the positions of the occultists who hold that the phenomena of Mind are likewise modes of vibration or motion. Let us see what science has to say regarding the question of vibrations in matter and energy.

In the first place, science teaches that all matter manifests, in some degree, the vibrations arising from temperature or heat. Be an object cold or hot—both being but degrees of the same things—it manifests certain heat vibrations, and in that sense is in motion and vibration. Then all particles of Matter are in circular movement, from corpuscle to suns. The planets revolve around suns, and many of them turn on their axes. The suns move around greater central points, and these are believed to move around still greater, and so on, ad infinitum. The molecules of which the particular kinds of Matter are composed are in a state of constant vibration and movement around each other and against each other. The molecules are composed of Atoms, which, likewise, are in a state of constant movement and vibration. The atoms are composed of Corpuscles, sometimes called "electrons," "ions," etc., which also are in a state of rapid motion, revolving around each other, and which manifest a very rapid state and mode of vibration. And, so we see that all forms of Matter manifest Vibration, in accordance with the Hermetic Principle of Vibration.

And so it is with the various forms of Energy. Science teaches that Light, Heat, Magnetism and Electricity are but forms of vibratory motion connected in some way with, and probably emanating from the Ether. Science does not as yet attempt to explain the nature of the phenomena known as Cohesion, which is the principle of Molecular Attraction; nor Chemical Affinity, which is the principle of Atomic Attraction; nor Gravitation (the greatest mystery of the three), which is the principle of attraction by which every particle or mass of Matter is bound to every other particle or mass. These three forms of Energy are not as yet understood by science, yet the writers incline to the opinion that these too are manifestations of some form of vibratory energy, a fact which the Hermetists have held and taught for ages past.

The Universal Ether, which is postulated by science without its nature being understood clearly, is held by the Hermetists to be but a higher manifestation of that which is erroneously called matter—that is to say, Matter at a higher degree of vibration—and is called by them "The Ethereal Substance." The Hermetists teach that this Ethereal Substance is of extreme tenuity and elasticity, and pervades universal space, serving as a medium of transmission of waves of vibratory energy, such as heat, light, electricity, magnetism, etc. The Teachings are that The Ethereal Substance is a connecting link between the forms of vibratory energy known as "Matter" on the one hand, and "Energy or

Force" on the other; and also that it manifests a degree of vibration, in rate and mode, entirely its own.

Scientists have offered the illustration of a rapidly moving wheel, top, or cylinder, to show the effects of increasing rates of vibration. The illustration supposes a wheel, top, or revolving cylinder, running at a low rate of speed—we will call this revolving thing "the object" in following out the illustration. Let us suppose the object moving slowly. It may be seen readily, but no sound of its movement reaches the ear. The speed is gradually increased. In a few moments its movement becomes so rapid that a deep growl or low note may be heard. Then as the rate is increased the note rises one in the musical scale. Then, the motion being still further increased, the next highest note is distinguished. Then, one after another, all the notes of the musical scale appear, rising higher and higher as the motion is increased. Finally when the motions have reached a certain rate the final note perceptible to human ears is reached and the shrill, piercing shriek dies away, and silence follows. No sound is heard from the revolving object, the rate of motion being so high that the human ear cannot register the vibrations. Then comes the perception of rising degrees of Heat. Then after quite a time the eye catches a glimpse of the object becoming a dull dark reddish color. As the rate increases, the red becomes brighter. Then as the speed is increased, the red melts into an orange. Then the orange melts into a yellow. Then follow, successively, the shades of green, blue, indigo, and finally violet, as the rate of sped increases. Then the violet shades away, and all color disappears, the human eye not being able to register them. But there are invisible rays emanating from the revolving object, the rays that are used in photographing, and other subtle rays of light. Then begin to manifest the peculiar rays known as the "X Rays," etc., as the constitution of the object changes. Electricity and

Magnetism are emitted when the appropriate rate of vibration is attained.

When the object reaches a certain rate of vibration its molecules disintegrate, and resolve themselves into the original elements or atoms. Then the atoms, following the Principle of Vibration, are separated into the countless corpuscles of which they are composed. And finally, even the corpuscles disappear and the object may be said to Be composed of The Ethereal Substance. Science does not dare to follow the illustration further, but the Hermetists teach that if the vibrations be continually increased the object would mount up the successive states of manifestation and would in turn manifest the various mental stages, and then on Spiritward, until it would finally re-enter THE ALL, which is Absolute Spirit. The "object," however, would have ceased to be an "object" long before the stage of Ethereal Substance was reached, but otherwise the illustration is correct inasmuch as it shows the effect of constantly increased rates and modes of vibration. It must be remembered, in the above illustration, that at the stages at which the "object" throws off vibrations of light, heat, etc., it is not actually "resolved" into those forms of energy (which are much higher in the scale), but simply that it reaches a degree of vibration in which those forms of energy are liberated, in a degree, from the confining influences of its molecules, atoms and corpuscles, as the case may be. These forms of energy, although much higher in the scale than matter, are imprisoned and confined in the material combinations, by reason of the energies manifesting through, and using material forms, but thus becoming entangled and confined in their creations of material forms, which, to an extent, is true of all creations, the creating force becoming involved in its creation.

But the Hermetic Teachings go much further than do those of modern science. They teach that all manifestation of thought, emotion, reason, will or desire, or any mental state or condition, are accompanied by vibrations, a portion of which are thrown off and which tend to affect the minds of other persons by "induction." This is the principle which produces the phenomena of "telepathy"; mental influence, and other forms of the action and power of mind over mind, with which the general public is rapidly becoming acquainted, owing to the wide dissemination of occult knowledge by the various schools, cults and teachers along these lines at this time.

Every thought, emotion or mental state has its corresponding rate and mode of vibration. And by an effort of the will of the person, or of other persons, these mental states may be reproduced, just as a musical tone may be reproduced by causing an instrument to vibrate at a certain rate—just as color may be reproduced in the same may. By a knowledge of the Principle of Vibration, as applied to Mental Phenomena, one may polarize his mind at any degree he wishes, thus gaining a perfect control over his mental states, moods, etc. In the same way he may affect the minds of others, producing the desired mental states in them. In short, he may be able to produce on the Mental Plane that which science produces on the Physical Plane—namely, "Vibrations at Will." This power of course may be acquired only by the proper instruction, exercises, practice, etc., the science being that of Mental Transmutation, one of the branches of the Hermetic Art.

A little reflection on what we have said will show the student that the Principle of Vibration underlies the wonderful phenomena of the power manifested by the Masters and Adepts, who are able to apparently set aside the Laws of Nature, but who, in reality, are simply using one law against another; one principle against others; and who accomplish their results by changing the vibrations of material objects, or forms of energy, and thus perform what are commonly called "miracles."

As one of the old Hermetic writers has truly said: "He who understands the Principle of Vibration, has grasped the scepter of Power."

10

POLARITY

"Everything is dual; everything has poles; everything has its pair of opposites; like and unlike are the same; opposites are identical in nature, but different in degree; extremes meet; all truths are but half-truths; all paradoxes may be reconciled."

— THE KYBALION.

The great Fourth Hermetic Principle—the Principle of Polarity embodies the truth that all manifested things have "two sides"; "two aspects"; "two poles"; a "pair of opposites," with manifold degrees between the two extremes. The old paradoxes, which have ever perplexed the mind of men, are explained by an understanding of this Principle. Man has always recognized something akin to this Principle, and has endeavored to express it by such sayings, maxims and aphorisms as the following: "Everything is and isn't, at the same time"; "all truths are but half-truths"; "every truth is half-false"; "there are two sides to everything"—"there is a reverse side to every shield," etc., etc.

The Hermetic Teachings are to the effect that the difference between things seemingly diametrically opposed to each other is merely a matter of degree. It teaches that "the pairs of opposites may be reconciled," and that "thesis and anti-thesis are identical in nature, but different in degree"; and that the "universal reconciliation of opposites" is effected by a recognition of this Principle of Polarity. The teachers claim that illustrations of this Principle may be had on every hand, and from an examination into the real nature of anything. They begin by showing that Spirit and Matter are but the two poles of the same thing, the intermediate planes being merely degrees of vibration. They show that THE ALL and The Many are the same, the difference being merely a matter of degree of Mental Manifestation. Thus the LAW and Laws are the two opposite poles of one thing. Likewise, PRINCIPLE and Principles. Infinite Mind and finite minds.

Then passing on to the Physical Plane, they illustrate the Principle by showing that Heat and Cold are identical in nature, the differences being merely a matter of degrees. The thermometer shows many degrees of temperature, the lowest pole being called "cold," and the highest "heat." Between these two poles are many degrees of "heat" or "cold," call them either and you are equally correct. The higher of two degrees is always "warmer," while the lower is always "colder." There is no absolute standard-all is a matter of degree. There is no place on the thermometer where heat ceases and cold begins. It is all a matter of higher or lower vibrations. The very terms "high" and "low," which we are compelled to use, are but poles of the same thing-the terms are relative. So with "East and West"—travel around the world in an eastward direction, and you reach a point which is called west at your starting point, and you return from that westward point.

Travel far enough North, and you will find yourself traveling South, or vice versa.

Light and Darkness are poles of the same thing, with many degrees between them. The musical scale is the same—starting with "C" you move upward until you reach another "C" and so on, the differences between the two ends of the board being the same, with many degrees between the two extremes. The scale of color is the same-higher and lower vibrations being the only difference between high violet and low red. Large and Small are relative. So are Noise and Quiet; Hard and Soft follow the rule. Likewise Sharp and Dull. Positive and Negative are two poles of the same thing, with countless degrees between them.

Good and Bad are not absolute—we call one end of the scale Good and the other Bad, or one end Good and the other Evil, according to the use of the terms. A thing is "less good" than the thing higher in the scale; but that "less good" thing, in turn, is "more good" than the thing next below it—and so on, the "more or less" being regulated by the position on the scale.

And so it is on the Mental Plane. "Love and. Hate" are generally regarded as being things diametrically opposed to each other; entirely different; unreconcilable. But we apply the Principle of Polarity; we find that there is no such thing as Absolute Love or Absolute Hate, as distinguished from each other. The two are merely terms applied to the two poles of the same thing. Beginning at any point of the scale we find "more love," or "less hate," as we ascend the scale; and "more hate" or "less love" as we descend this being true no matter from what point, high or low, we may start. There are degrees of Love and Hate, and there is a middle point where "Like and Dislike" become so faint that it is difficult to distinguish between them. Courage and Fear come under the same rule. The Pairs of Opposites exist everywhere. Where you find one thing you find its opposite-the two poles.

And it is this fact that enables the Hermetist to transmute one mental state into another, along the lines of Polarization. Things belonging to different classes cannot be transmuted into each other, but things of the same class may be changed, that is, may have their polarity changed. Thus Love never becomes East or West, or Red or Violet-but it may and often does turn into Hate and likewise Hate may be transformed into Love, by changing its polarity. Courage may be transmuted into Fear, and the reverse. Hard things may be rendered Soft. Dull things become Sharp. Hot things become Cold. And so on, the transmutation always being between things of the same kind of different degrees. Take the case of a Fearful man. By raising his mental vibrations along the line of Fear- Courage, he can be filled with the highest degree of Courage and Fearlessness. And, likewise, the Slothful man may change himself into an Active, Energetic individual simply by polarizing along the lines of the desired quality.

The student who is familiar with the processes by which the various schools of Mental Science, etc., produce changes in the mental states of those following their teachings, may not readily understand the principle underlying many of these changes. When, however, the Principle of Polarity is once grasped, and it is seen that the mental changes are occasioned by a change of polarity-a sliding along the same scale-the hatter is readily understood. The change is not in the nature of a transmutation of one thing into another thing entirely different-but is merely a change of degree in the same things, a vastly important difference. For instance, borrowing an analogy from the Physical Plane, it is impossible to change Heat into Sharpness, Loudness, Highness, etc., but Heat may readily be transmuted into Cold, simply by lowering the vibrations. In the same way Hate and

Love are mutually transmutable; so are Fear and Courage. But Fear cannot be transformed into Love, nor can Courage be transmuted into Hate. The mental states belong to innumerable classes, each class of which has its opposite poles, along which transmutation is possible.

The student will readily recognize that in the mental states, as well as in the phenomena of the Physical Plane, the two poles may be classified as Positive and Negative, respectively. Thus Love is Positive to Hate; Courage to Fear; Activity to Non-Activity, etc., etc. And it will also be noticed that even to those unfamiliar with the Principle of Vibration, the Positive pole seems to be of a higher degree than the Negative, and readily dominates it. The tendency of Nature is in the direction of the dominant activity of the Positive pole.

In addition to the changing of the poles of one's own mental states by the operation of the art of Polarization, the phenomena of Mental Influence, in its manifold phases, shows us that the principle may be extended so as to embrace the phenomena of the influence of one mind over that of another, of which so much has been written and taught of late years. When it is understood that Mental Induction is possible, that is that mental states may be produced by "induction" from others, then we can readily see how a certain rate of vibration, or polarization of a certain mental state, may be communicated to another person, and his polarity in that class of mental states thus changed. It is along this principle that the results of many of the "mental treatments" are obtained. For instance, a person is "blue," melancholy and full of fear. A mental scientist bringing his own mind up to the desired vibration by his trained will, and thus obtaining the desired polarization in his own case, then produces a similar mental state in the other by induction, the result being that the vibrations are raised and the person polarizes toward the Positive end of the scale instead toward the Negative, and his Fear and other negative emotions are transmuted to Courage and similar positive mental states. A little study will show you that these mental changes are nearly all along the line of Polarization, the change being one of degree rather than of kind.

A knowledge of the existence of this great Hermetic Principle will enable the student to better understand his own mental states, and those of other people. He will see that these states are all matters of degree, and seeing thus, he will be able to raise or lower the vibration at will—to change his mental poles, and thus be Master of his mental states, instead of being their servant and slave. And by his knowledge he will be able to aid his fellows intelligently and by the appropriate methods change the polarity when the same is desirable. We advise all students to familiarize themselves with this Principle of Polarity, for a correct understanding of the same will throw light on many difficult subjects.

II
RHYTHM

> *"Everything flows out and in; everything has its tides; all things rise and fall; the pendulum-swing manifests in everything; the measure of the swing to the right, is the measure of the swing to the left; rhythm compensates"*
>
> — THE KYBALION.

The great Fifth Hermetic Principle—the Principle of Rhythm-embodies the truth that in everything there is manifested a measured motion; a to-and-from movement; a flow and inflow; a swing forward and backward; a pendulum-like movement; a tide-like ebb and flow; a high-tide and a low- tide; between the two-poles manifest on the physical, mental or spiritual planes. The Principle of rhythm is closely connected with the Principle of Polarity described in the preceding chapter. Rhythm manifests between the two poles established by the Principle of Polarity. This does not mean, however, that the pendulum of Rhythm swings to the extreme poles, for this rarely happens; in fact, it is difficult to establish the extreme polar opposites in the majority of cases. But the swing is ever "toward" first one pole and then the other.

There is always an action and reaction; an advance and a retreat; a rising and a sinking; manifested in all of the airs and phenomena of the Universe. Suns, worlds, men, animals, plants, minerals, forces, energy, mind and matter, yes, even Spirit, manifests this Principle. The Principle manifests in the creation and destruction of worlds; in the rise and fall of nations; in the life history of all things; and finally in the mental states of Man.

Beginning with the manifestations of Spirit—of THE ALL—it will be noticed that there is ever the Outpouring and the Indrawing; the "Outbreathing and Inbreathing of Brahm," as the Brahmans word it. Universes are created; reach their extreme low point of materiality; and then begin in their upward swing. Suns spring into being, and then their height of power being reached, the process of retrogression begins, and after aeons they become dead masses of matter, awaiting another impulse which starts again their inner energies into activity and a new solar life cycle is begun. And thus it is with all the worlds; they are born, grow and die; only to be reborn. And thus it is with all the things of shape and form; they swing from action to reaction; from birth to death; from activity to inactivity—and then back again. Thus it is with all living things; they are born, grow, and die—and then are reborn. So it is with all great movements, philosophies, creeds, fashions, governments, nations, and all else-birth, growth, maturity, decadence, death-and then new-birth. The swing of the pendulum is ever in evidence.

Night follows day; and day night. The pendulum swings from Summer to Winter, and then back again. The corpuscles, atoms, molecules, and all masses of matter, swing around the circle of their nature. There is no such thing as absolute rest, or cessation from movement, and all movement partakes of rhythm. The principle is of universal application. It may be applied to any question, or phenomena of any of the many planes of life. It may be applied to all phases of human activity. There is always the Rhythmic swing from one pole to the other. The Universal Pendulum is ever in motion. The Tides of Life flow in and out, according to Law.

The Principle of rhythm is well understood by modern science, and is considered a universal law as applied to material things. But the Hermetists carry the principle much further, and know that its manifestations and influence extend to the mental activities of Man, and that it accounts for the bewildering succession of moods, feelings and other annoying and perplexing changes that we notice in ourselves. But the Hermetists by studying the operations of this Principle have learned to escape some of its activities by Transmutation.

The Hermetic Masters long since discovered that while the Principle of Rhythm was invariable, and ever in evidence in mental phenomena, still there were two planes of its manifestation so far as mental phenomena are concerned. They discovered that there were two general planes of Consciousness, the Lower and the Higher, the understanding of which fact enabled them to rise to the higher plane and thus escape the swing of the Rhythmic pendulum which manifested on the lower plane. In other words, the swing of the pendulum occurred on the Unconscious Plane, and the Consciousness was not affected. This they call the Law of Neutralization. Its operations consist in the raising of the Ego above the vibrations of the Unconscious Plane of mental activity, so that the negative-swing of the pendulum is not manifested in consciousness, and therefore they are not affected. It is akin to rising above a thing and letting it pass beneath you. The Hermetic Master, or advanced student, polarizes himself at the desired pole, and by a process akin to "refusing" to participate in the backward swing or, if you prefer, a "denial" of its influence over him, he stands firm in his polarized position, and allows the mental pendulum to swing back along the unconscious plane. All individuals who have attained any degree of self- mastery, accomplish this, more or less unknowingly, and by refusing to allow their moods and negative mental states to affect them, they apply the Law of Neutralization. The Master, however, carries this to a much higher degree of proficiency, and by the use of his Will he attains a degree of Poise and Mental Firmness almost impossible of belief on the part of those who allow themselves to be swung backward and forward by the mental pendulum of moods and feelings.

The importance of this will be appreciated by any thinking person who realizes what creatures of moods, feelings and emotion the majority of people are, and how little mastery of themselves they manifest. If you will stop and consider a moment, you will realize how much these swings of Rhythm have affected you in your life—how a period of Enthusiasm has been invariably followed by an opposite feeling and mood of Depression. Likewise, your moods and periods of Courage have been succeeded by equal moods of Fear. And so it has ever been with the majority of persons—tides of feeling have ever risen and fallen with them, but they have never suspected the cause or reason of the mental phenomena. An understanding of the workings of this Principle will give one the key to the Mastery of these rhythmic swings of feeling, and will enable him to know himself better and to avoid being carried away by these inflows and outflows. The Will is superior to the conscious manifestation of this Principle, although the Principle itself can never be destroyed. We may escape its effects, but the Principle operates, nevertheless. The pendulum ever swings, although we may escape being carried along with it.

There are other features of the operation of this Principle of Rhythm of which we wish to speak at this point. There comes into its operations that which is known as the Law of Compensation. One of the definitions or meanings of the word "Compensate" is, "to counterbalance" which is the sense in which the Hermetists use the term. It is this Law of Compensation to which the Kybalion refers when it says: "The measure of the swing to the right is the measure of the swing to the left; rhythm compensates."

The Law of Compensation is that the swing in one direction determines the swing in the opposite direction, or to the opposite pole-the one balances, or counterbalances, the other. On the Physical Plane we see many examples of this Law. The pendulum of the clock swings a certain distance to the right, and then an equal distance to the left. The seasons balance each other in the same way. The tides follow the same Law. And the same Law is manifested in all the phenomena of Rhythm. The pendulum, with a short swing in one direction, has but a short swing in the other; while the long swing to the right invariably means the long swing to the left. An object hurled upward to a certain height has an equal distance to traverse on its return. The force with which a projectile is sent upward a mile is reproduced when the projectile returns to the earth on its return journey. This Law is constant on the Physical Plane, as reference to the standard authorities will show you.

But the Hermetists carry it still further. They teach that a man's mental states are subject to the same Law. The man who enjoys keenly, is subject to keen suffering; while he who feels but little pain is capable of feeling but little joy. The pig suffers but little mentally, and enjoys but little—he is compensated. And on the other hand, there are other animals who enjoy keenly, but whose nervous organism and temperament cause them to suffer exquisite degrees of pain and so it is with Man. There are temperaments which permit of but low degrees of enjoyment, and equally low degrees of suffering; while there are others which permit the most intense enjoyment, but also the most intense suffering. The rule is that the capacity for pain and pleasure, in each individual, are balanced. The Law of Compensation is in full operation here.

But the Hermetists go still further in this matter. They teach that before one is able to enjoy a certain degree of pleasure, he must have swung as far, proportionately, toward the other pole of feeling. They hold, however, that the Negative is precedent to the Positive in this matter, that is to say that in experiencing a certain degree of pleasure it does not follow that he will have to "pay up for it" with a corresponding degree of pain; on the contrary, the pleasure is the Rhythmic swing, according to the Law of Compensation, for a degree of pain previously experienced either in the present life, or in a previous incarnation. This throws a new light on the Problem of Pain.

The Hermetists regard the chain of lives as continuous, and as forming a part of one life of the individual, so that in consequence the rhythmic swing is understood in this way, while it would be without meaning unless the truth of reincarnation is admitted.

But the Hermetists claim that the Master or advanced student is able, to a great degree, to escape the swing toward Pain, by the process of Neutralization before mentioned. By rising on to the higher plane of the Ego, much of the experience that comes to those dwelling on the lower plane is avoided and escaped.

The Law of Compensation plays an important part in the lives of men and women. It will be noticed that one generally "pays the price" of anything he possesses or lacks. If he has one thing, he lacks another—the balance is struck. No one can "keep his penny and have the bit of cake" at the same time Everything has its pleasant and unpleasant sides. The things that one gains are always paid for by the things that one loses. The rich possess much that the poor lack, while the poor often possess things that are beyond the reach of the rich. The millionaire may have the inclination toward feasting, and the wealth wherewith to secure all the dainties and luxuries of the table, while he lacks the appetite to enjoy the same; he envies the appetite and digestion of the laborer who lacks the wealth and inclinations of the millionaire, and who gets more pleasure from his plain food than the millionaire could obtain even if his appetite were not jaded, nor his digestion ruined, for the wants, habits and inclinations differ. And so it is through life. The Law of Compensation is ever in operation, striving to balance and counter-balance, and always succeeding in time, even though several lives may be required for the return swing of the Pendulum of Rhythm.

12

CAUSATION

> *"Every Cause has its Effect; every Effect has its Cause; everything happens according to Law; Chance is but a name for Law not recognized; there are many planes of causation, but nothing escapes the Law."*
>
> — THE KYBALION.

The great Sixth Hermetic Principle—the Principle of Cause and Effect—embodies the truth that Law pervades the Universe; that nothing happens by Chance; that Chance is merely a term indicating cause existing but not recognized or perceived; that phenomena is continuous, without break or exception.

The Principle of Cause and Effect underlies all scientific thought, ancient and modern, and was enunciated by the Hermetic Teachers in the earliest days. While many and varied disputes between the many schools of thought have since arisen, these disputes have been principally upon the details of the operations of the Principle, and still more often upon the meaning of certain words. The underlying Principle of Cause and Effect has been accepted as correct by practically all the thinkers of the world worthy of the name. To think otherwise would be to take the phenomena of the universe from the domain of Law and Order, and to relegate it; to the control of the imaginary something which men have called "Chance."

A little consideration will show anyone that there is in reality no such thing as pure chance. Webster defines the word "Chance" as follows: "A supposed agent or mode of activity other than a force, law or purpose; the operation or activity of such agent; the supposed effect of such an agent; a happening; fortuity; casualty, etc." But a little consideration will show you that there can be no such agent as "Chance," in the sense of something outside of Law-something outside of Cause and Effect. How could there be a something acting in the phenomenal universe, independent of the laws, order, and continuity of the latter? Such a something would be entirely independent of the orderly trend of the universe, and therefore superior to it. We can imagine nothing outside of THE ALL being outside of the Law, and that only because THE ALL is the LAW in itself. There is no room in the universe for a something outside of and independent of Law. The existence of such a Something would render all Natural Laws ineffective, and would plunge the universe into chaotic disorder and lawlessness.

A careful examination will show that what we call "Chance" is merely an expression relating to obscure causes; causes that we cannot perceive; causes that we cannot understand. The word Chance is derived from a word Meaning "to fall" (as the falling of dice), the idea being that the fall of the dice (and many other happenings) are merely a "happening" unrelated to any cause. And this is the sense in which the term is generally employed. But when the matter is closely examined, it is seen that there is no chance whatsoever about the fall of the dice. Each time a die falls, and displays a certain number, it obeys a law as infallible as that which governs the revolution of the planets around the sun. Back of the fall of the die are causes, or chains of causes, running back further than the mind can follow. The position of the die in the box; the amount of muscular energy expended in the throw; the condition of the table, etc., etc., all are causes, the effect of which may be seen. But back of these seen causes there are chains of unseen preceding causes, all of which had a bearing upon the number of the die which fell uppermost.

If a die be cast a great number of times, it will be found that the numbers shown will be about equal, that is, there will be an equal number of one-spot, two-spot, etc., coming uppermost. Toss a penny in the air, and it may come down either "heads" or "tails"; but make a sufficient number of tosses, and the heads and tails will about even up. This is the operation of the law of average. But both the average and the single toss come under the Law of Cause and Effect, and if we were able to examine into the preceding causes, it would be clearly seen that it was simply impossible for the die to fall other than it did, under the same circumstances and at the same time. Given the same causes, the same results will follow. There is always a "cause" and a "because" to every event. Nothing ever "happens" without a cause, or rather a chain of causes.

Some confusion has arisen in the minds of persons considering this Principle, from the fact that they were unable to explain how one thing could cause another thing—that is, be the "creator" of the second thing. As a matter of fact, no "thing" ever causes or "creates" another "thing." Cause and Effect deals merely with "events." An "event" is "that which comes, arrives or happens, as a result or consequent of some preceding event." No event "creates" another event, but is merely a preceding link in the great orderly chain of events flowing from the creative energy of THE ALL. There is a continuity between all events precedent, consequent and subsequent. There is a relation existing between everything that has gone before, and everything that follows. A stone is dislodged from a mountain side and crashes through a roof of a cottage in the valley below. At first sight we regard this as a chance effect, but when we examine the matter we find a great chain of causes behind it. In the first place there was the rain which softened the earth supporting the stone and which allowed it to fall; then back of that was the influence of the sun, other rains, etc., which gradually disintegrated the piece of rock from a larger piece; then there were the causes which led to the formation of the mountain, and its upheaval by convulsions of nature, and so on ad infinitum. Then we might follow up the causes behind the rain, etc. Then we might consider the existence of the roof In short, we would soon find ourselves involved in a mesh of cause and effect, from which we would soon strive to extricate ourselves.

Just as a man has two parents, and four grandparents, and eight great-grandparents, and sixteen great-great-grandparents, and so on until when, say, forty generations are calculated the numbers of ancestors run into many millions—so it is with the number of causes behind even the most trifling event or phenomena, such as the passage of a tiny speck of soot before your eye. It is not an easy matter to trace the bit of soot hack to the early period of the world's history when it formed a part of a massive tree-trunk, which was afterward converted into coal, and so on, until as the speck of soot it now passes before your vision on its way to other adventures. And a mighty chain of events, causes and effects, brought it to its present condition, and the later is but one of the chain of events which will go to produce other events hundreds of years from now. One of the series of events arising from the tiny bit of soot was the writing of these lines, which caused the typesetter to perform certain work; the proofreader to do likewise; and which will arouse certain thoughts in your mind, and that of others, which in turn will affect others, and so on, and on, and on, beyond the ability of man to think further-and all from the passage of a tiny bit of soot, all of which shows the relativity and association of things, and the further fact that "there is no great; there is no small, in the mind that causeth all."

Stop to think a moment. If a certain man had not met a certain maid, away back in the dim period of the Stone Age—you who are now reading these lines would not now be here. And if, perhaps, the same couple had failed to meet, we who now write these lines would not now be here. And the very act of writing, on our part, and the act of reading, on yours, will affect not only the respective lives of yourself and ourselves, but will also have a direct, or indirect, affect upon many other people now living and who will live in the ages to come. Every thought we think, every act we perform, has its direct and indirect results which fit into the great chain of Cause and Effect.

We do not wish to enter into a consideration of Free Will, or Determinism, in this work, for various reasons. Among the many reasons, is the principal one that neither side of the controversy is entirely right-in fact, both sides are partially right, according to the Hermetic Teachings. The Principle of Polarity shows that both are but Half-Truths the opposing poles of Truth. The Teachings are that a man may be both Free and yet bound by Necessity, depending upon the meaning of the terms, and the height of Truth from which the matter is examined. The ancient writers express the matter thus: "The further the creation is from the Centre, the more it is bound; the nearer the Centre it reaches, the nearer Free is it."

The majority of people are more or less the slaves of heredity, environment, etc., and manifest very little Freedom. They are swayed by the opinions, customs and thoughts of the outside world, and also by their emotions, feelings, moods, etc. They manifest no Mastery, worthy of the name. They indignantly repudiate this assertion, saying, "Why, I certainly am free to act and do as I please—I do just what I want to do," but they fail to explain whence arise the "want to" and "as I please." What makes them "want to" do one thing in preference to another; what makes them "please" to do this, and not do that? Is there no "because" to their "pleasing" and "Wanting"? The Master can change these "pleases" and "wants" into others at the opposite end of the mental pole. He is able to "Will to will," instead of to will because some feeling, mood, emotion, or environmental suggestion arouses a tendency or desire within him so to do.

The majority of people are carried along like the falling stone, obedient to environment, outside influences and internal moods, desires, etc., not to speak of the desires and wills of others stronger than themselves, heredity, environment, and suggestion, carrying them along without resistance on their part, or the exercise of the Will. Moved like the pawns on the checkerboard of life, they play their parts and are laid aside after the game is over. But the Masters, knowing the rules of the game, rise above the plane of material life, and placing themselves in touch with the higher powers of their nature, dominate their own moods, characters, qualities, and polarity, as well as the environment surrounding them and thus become Movers in the game, instead of Pawns-Causes instead of Effects. The Masters do not escape the Causation of the higher planes, but fall in with the higher laws, and thus master circumstances on the lower plane. They thus form a conscious part of the Law, instead of being mere blind instruments.

While they Serve on the Higher Planes, they Rule on the Material Plane.

But, on higher and on lower, the Law is always in operation. There is no such thing as Chance. The blind goddess has been abolished by Reason. We are able to see now, with eyes made clear by knowledge, that everything is governed by Universal Law-that the infinite number of laws are but manifestations of the One Great Law-the LAW which is THE ALL. It is true indeed that not a sparrow drops unnoticed by the Mind of THE AL—that even the hairs on our head are numbered—as the scriptures have said There is nothing outside of Law; nothing that happens contrary to it. And yet, do not make the mistake of supposing that Man is but a blind automaton-far from that. The Hermetic Teachings are that Man may use Law to overcome laws, and that the higher will always prevail against the lower, until at last he has reached the stage in which he seeks refuge in the LAW itself, and laughs the phenomenal laws to scorn. Are you able to grasp the inner meaning of this?

13
GENDER

"Gender is in everything; everything has its Masculine and Feminine Principles; Gender manifests on all planes."

— THE KYBALION.

The great Seventh Hermetic Principle—the Principle of Gender-embodies the truth that there is Gender manifested in everything-that the Masculine and Feminine principles are ever present and active in all phases of phenomena, on each and every plane of life. At this point we think it well to call your attention to the fact that Gender, in its Hermetic sense, and Sex in the ordinarily accepted use of the term, are not the same.

The word "Gender" is derived from the Latin root meaning "to beget; to procreate; to generate; to create; to produce." A moment's consideration will show you that the word has a much broader and more general meaning than the term "Sex," the latter referring to the physical distinctions between male and female living things. Sex is merely a manifestation of Gender on a certain plane of the Great Physical Plane—the plane of organic life. We wish to impress this distinction upon your minds, for the reason that certain writers, who have acquired a smattering of the Hermetic Philosophy, have sought to identify this Seventh Hermetic Principle with wild and fanciful, and often reprehensible, theories and teachings regarding Sex.

The office of Gender is solely that of creating, producing, generating, etc., and its manifestations are visible on every plane of phenomena. It is somewhat difficult to produce proofs of this along scientific lines, for the reason that science has not as yet recognized this Principle as of universal application. But still some proofs are forthcoming from scientific sources. In the first place, we find a distinct manifestation of the Principle of Gender among the corpuscles, ions, or electrons, which constitute the basis of Matter as science now knows the latter, and which by forming certain combinations form the Atom, which until lately was regarded as final and indivisible.

The latest word of science is that the atom is composed of a multitude of corpuscles, electrons, or ions (the various names being applied by different authorities) revolving around each other and vibrating at a high degree and intensity. But the accompanying statement is made that the formation of the atom is really due to the clustering of negative corpuscles around a positive one—the positive corpuscles seeming to exert a certain influence upon the negative corpuscles, causing the latter to assume certain combinations and thus "create" or "generate" an atom. This is in line with the most ancient Hermetic Teachings, which have always identified the Masculine principle of Gender with the "Positive," and the Feminine with the "Negative" Poles of Electricity (so called).

Now a word at this point regarding this identification. The public mind has formed an entirely erroneous impression regarding the qualities of the so-called "Negative" pole of electrified or magnetized Matter. The terms Positive and Negative are very wrongly applied to this phenomenon by science. The word Positive means something real and strong, as compared with a Negative unreality or weakness. Nothing is further from the real facts of electrical phenomenon. The so-called Negative pole of the battery is really the pole in and by which the generation or production of new forms and energies is manifested. There is nothing "negative" about it. The best scientific authorities now use the word "Cathode" in place of "Negative," the word Cathode coming from the Greek root meaning "descent; the path of generation, etc.," From the Cathode pole emerge the swarm of electrons or corpuscles; from the same pole emerge those wonderful "rays" which have revolutionized scientific conceptions during the past decade. The Cathode pole is the Mother of all of the strange phenomena which have rendered useless the old textbooks, and which have caused many long accepted theories to be relegated to the scrap-pile of scientific speculation. The Cathode, or Negative Pole, is the Mother Principle of Electrical Phenomena, and of the finest forms of matter as yet known to science. So you see we are justified in refusing to use the term "Negative" in our consideration of the subject, and in insisting upon substituting the word "Feminine" for the old term. The facts of the case bear us out in this, without taking the Hermetic Teachings into consideration. And so we shall use the word "Feminine" in the place of "Negative" in speaking of that pole of activity.

The latest scientific teachings are that the creative corpuscles or electrons are Feminine (science says "they are composed of negative electricity"-we say they are composed of Feminine energy).

A Feminine corpuscle becomes detached from, or rather leaves, a Masculine corpuscle, and starts on a new career. It actively seeks a union with a Masculine corpuscle, being urged thereto by the natural impulse to create new forms of Matter or Energy. One writer goes so far as to use the term "it at once seeks, of its own volition, a union," etc. This detachment and uniting form the basis of the greater part of the activities of the chemical world. When the Feminine corpuscle unites with a Masculine corpuscle, a certain process is begun. The Feminine particles vibrate rapidly under the influence of the Masculine energy, and circle rapidly around the latter. The result is the birth of a new atom. This new atom is really composed of a union of the Masculine and Feminine electrons, or corpuscles, but when the union is formed the atom is a separate thing, having certain properties, but no longer manifesting the property of free electricity. The process of detachment or separation of the Feminine electrons is called "ionization." These electrons, or corpuscles, are the most active workers in Nature's field. Arising from their unions, or combinations, manifest the varied phenomena of light, heat, electricity, magnetism, attraction, repulsion, chemical affinity and the reverse, and similar phenomena. And all this arises from the operation of the Principle of Gender on the plane of Energy.

The part of the Masculine principle seems to be that of directing a certain inherent energy toward the Feminine principle, and thus starting into activity the creative processes. But the Feminine principle is the one always doing the active creative work—and this is so on all planes. And yet, each principle is incapable of operative energy without the assistance of the other. In some of the forms of life, the two principles are combined in one organism. For that matter, everything in the organic world manifests both genders—there is always the Masculine present in the

Feminine form, and the Feminine form. The Hermetic Teachings include much regarding the operation of the two principles of Gender in the production and manifestation of various forms of energy, etc., but we do not deem it expedient to go into detail regarding the same at this point, because we are unable to back up the same with scientific proof, for the reason that science has not as yet progressed thus far. But the example we have given you of the phenomena of the electrons or corpuscles will show you that science is on the right path, and will also give you a general idea of the underlying principles.

Some leading scientific investigators have announced their belief that in the formation of crystals there was to be found something that corresponded to "sex-activity" which is another straw showing the direction the scientific winds are blowing. And each year will bring other facts to corroborate the correctness of the Hermetic Principle of Gender. It will be found that Gender is in constant operation and manifestation in the field of inorganic matter, and in the field of Energy or Force. Electricity is now generally regarded as the "Something" into which all other forms of energy seem to melt or dissolve. The "Electrical Theory of the Universe" is the latest scientific doctrine, and is growing rapidly in popularity and general acceptance. And it thus follows that if we are able to discover in the phenomena of electricity-even at the very root and source of its manifestations a clear and unmistakable evidence of the presence of Gender and its activities, we are justified in asking you to believe that science at last has offered proofs of the existence in all universal phenomena of that great Hermetic Principle-the Principle of Gender.

It is not necessary to take up your time with the well known phenomena of the "attraction and repulsion" of the atoms; chemical affinity; the "loves and hates" of the atomic particles; the attraction or cohesion between the molecules of matter.

These facts are too well known to need extended comment from us. But, have you ever considered that all of these things are manifestations of the Gender Principle? Can you not see that the phenomena is "on all fours" with that of the corpuscles or electrons? And more than this, can you not see the reasonableness of the Hermetic Teachings which assert that the very Law of Gravitation-that strange attraction by reason of which all particles and bodies of matter in the universe tend toward each other is but another manifestation of the Principle of Gender, which operates in the direction of attracting the Masculine to the Feminine energies, and vice versa? We cannot offer you scientific proof of this at this time-but examine the phenomena in the light of the Hermetic Teachings on the subject, and see if you have not a better working hypothesis than any offered by physical science. Submit all physical phenomena to the test, and you will discern the Principle of Gender ever in evidence.

Let us now pass on to a consideration of the operation of the Principle on the Mental Plane. Many interesting features are there awaiting examination.

14
MENTAL GENDER

Students of psychology who have followed the modern trend of thought along the lines of mental phenomena are struck by the persistence of the dual-mind idea which has manifested itself so strongly during the past ten or fifteen years, and which has given rise to a number of plausible theories regarding the nature and constitution of these "two minds." The late Thomson J. Hudson attained great popularity in 1893 by advancing his well-known theory of the "objective and subjective minds" which he held existed in every individual. Other writers have attracted almost equal attention by the theories regarding the "conscious and subconscious minds"; the "voluntary and involuntary minds"; "the active and passive minds," etc., etc. The theories of the various writers differ from each other, but there remains the underlying principle of "the duality of mind."

The student of the Hermetic Philosophy is tempted to smile when he reads and hears of these many "new theories" regarding the duality of mind, each school adhering tenaciously to its own pet theories, and each claiming to have "discovered the truth." The student turns back the pages of occult history, and away back in the dim beginnings of occult teachings he finds references to the ancient Hermetic doctrine of the Principle of Gender on the Mental Plane-the manifestation of Mental Gender. And examining further he finds that the ancient philosophy took cognizance of the phenomenon of the "dual mind," and accounted for it by the theory of Mental Gender. This idea of Mental Gender may be explained in a few words to students who are familiar with the modern theories just alluded to. The Masculine Principle of Mind corresponds to the so-called Objective Mind; Conscious Mind; Voluntary Mind; Active Mind, etc. And the Feminine Principle of Mind corresponds to the so-called Subjective Mind; Sub-conscious Mind; Involuntary Mind; Passive Mind, etc. Of course the Hermetic Teachings do not agree with the many modern theories regarding the nature of the two phases of mind, nor does it admit many of the facts claimed for the two respective aspects—some of the said theories and claims being very far-fetched and incapable of standing the test of experiment and demonstration. We point to the phases of agreement merely for the purpose of helping the student to assimilate his previously acquired knowledge with the teachings of the Hermetic Philosophy. Students of Hudson will notice the statement at the beginning of his second chapter of "The Law of Psychic Phenomena," that: "The mystic jargon of the Hermetic philosophers discloses the same general idea" i.e., the duality of mind. If Dr. Hudson had taken the time and trouble to decipher a little of "the mystic jargon of the Hermetic Philosophy," he might have received much light upon the subject of "the dual mind"—but then, perhaps, his most interesting work might not have been written. Let us now consider the Hermetic Teachings regarding Mental Gender.

The Hermetic Teachers impart their instruction regarding this subject by bidding their students examine the report of their consciousness regarding their Self. The students are bidden to turn their attention inward upon the Self dwelling within each. Each student is led to see that his consciousness gives him first a report of the existence of his Self-the report is "I Am." This at first seems to be the final words from the consciousness, but a little further examination discloses the fact that this "I Am" may be separated or split into two distinct parts, or aspects, which while working in unison and in conjunction, yet, nevertheless, may be separated in consciousness.

While at first there seems to be only an "I" existing, a more careful and closer examination reveals the fact that there exists an "I" and a "Me." These mental twins differ in their characteristics and nature, and an examination of their nature and the phenomena arising from the same will throw much light upon many of the problems of mental influence.

Let us begin with a consideration of the Me, which is usually mistaken for the I by the student, until he presses the inquiry a little further back into the recesses of consciousness. A man thinks of his Self (in its aspect of Me) as being composed of certain feelings, tastes likes, dislikes, habits, peculiar ties, characteristics, etc., all of which go to make up his personality, or the "Self" known to himself and others. He knows that these emotions and feelings change; are born and die away; are subject to the Principle of Rhythm, and the Principle of Polarity, which take him from one extreme of feeling to another. He also thinks of the "Me" as being certain knowledge gathered together in his mind, and thus forming a part of himself. This is the "Me" of a man.

But we have proceeded too hastily. The "Me" of many men may be said to consist largely of their consciousness of the body and their physical appetites, etc. Their consciousness being largely bound up with their bodily nature, they practically "live there." Some men even go so far as to regard their personal apparel as a part of their "Me" and actually seem to consider it a part of themselves. A writer has humorously said that "men consist of three parts—soul, body and clothes." These "clothes conscious" people would lose their personality if divested of their clothing by savages upon the occasion of a shipwreck. But even many who are not so closely bound up with the idea of personal raiment stick closely to the consciousness of their bodies being their "Me" They cannot conceive of a Self independent of the body. Their mind seems to them to be practically "a something belonging to" their body-which in many cases it is indeed.

But as man rises in the scale of consciousness he is able to disentangle his "Me" from his idea of body, and is able to think of his body as "belonging to" the mental part of him. But even then he is very apt to identify the "Me" entirely with the mental states, feelings, etc., which he feels to exist within him. He is very apt to consider these internal states as identical with himself, instead of their being simply "things" produced by some part of his mentality, and existing within him—of him, and in him, but still not "himself." He sees that he may change these internal states of feelings by all effort of will, and that he may produce a feeling or state of an exactly opposite nature, in the same way, and yet the same "Me" exists. And so after a while he is able to set aside these various mental states, emotions, feelings, habits, qualities, characteristics, and other personal mental belongings—he is able to set them aside in the "not-me" collection of curiosities and encumbrances, as well as valuable possessions. This requires much mental concentration and power of mental analysis on the part of the student. But still the task is possible for the advanced student, and even those not so far advanced are able to see, in the imagination, how the process may be performed.

After this laying-aside process has been performed, the student will find himself in conscious possession of a "Self" which may be considered in its "I" and "Me" dual aspects. The "Me" will be felt to be a Something mental in which thoughts, ideas, emotions, feelings, and other mental states may be produced. It may be considered as the "mental womb," as the ancients styled it-capable of generating mental offspring. It reports to the consciousness as a "Me" with latent powers of creation and generation of mental progeny of all sorts and kinds. Its powers of creative energy are felt to be enormous. But still it seems to be conscious that it must receive some form of energy from either its "I" companion, or else from some other "I" ere it is able to bring into being its mental creations. This consciousness brings with it a realization of an enormous capacity for mental work and creative ability.

But the student soon finds that this is not all that he finds within his inner consciousness. He finds that there exists a mental Something which is able to Will that the "Me" act along certain creative lines, and which is also able to stand aside and witness the mental creation. This part of himself he is taught to call his "I." He is able to rest in its consciousness at will. He finds there not a consciousness of an ability to generate and actively create, in the sense of the gradual process attendant upon mental operations, but rather a sense and consciousness of an ability to project an energy from the "I" to the "Me"—a process of "willing" that the mental creation begin and proceed. He also finds that the "I" is able to stand aside and witness the operations of the "Me's" mental creation and generation. There is this dual aspect in the mind of every person. The "I" represents the Masculine Principle of Mental Gender-the "Me" represents the Female Principle. The "I" represents the Aspect of Being; the "Me" the Aspect of Becoming. You will notice that the Principle of Correspondence operates on this plane just as it does upon the great plane upon which the creation of Universes is performed. The two are similar in kind, although vastly different in degree. "As above, so below; as below, so above."

These aspects of mind-the Masculine and Feminine Principles-the "I" and the "Me"-considered in connection with the well-known mental and psychic phenomena, give the master-key to these dimly known regions of mental operation and manifestation. The principle of Mental Gender gives the truth underlying the whole field of the phenomena of mental influence, etc.

The tendency of the Feminine Principle is always in the direction of receiving impressions, while the tendency of the Masculine Principle is always in the direction of giving, out or expressing. The Feminine Principle has much more varied field of operation than has the Masculine Principle. The Feminine Principle conducts the work of generating new thoughts, concepts, ideas, including the work of the imagination. The Masculine Principle contents itself with the work of the "Will" in its varied phases. And yet, without the active aid of the Will of the Masculine Principle, the Feminine Principle is apt to rest content with generating mental images which are the result of impressions received from outside, instead of producing original mental creations.

Persons who can give continued attention and thought to a subject actively employ both of the Mental Principles-the Feminine in the work of the mental generation, and the Masculine

Will in stimulating and energizing the creative portion of the mind. The majority of persons really employ the Masculine Principle but little, and are content to live according to the thoughts and ideas instilled into the "Me" from the "I" of other minds. But it is not our purpose to dwell upon this phase of the subject, which may be studied from any good text-book upon psychology, with the key that we have given you regarding Mental Gender.

The student of Psychic Phenomena is aware of the wonderful phenomena classified under the head of Telepathy; Thought Transference; Mental Influence; Suggestion; Hypnotism, etc. Many have sought for an explanation of these varied phases of phenomena under the theories of the various "dual mind" teachers. And in a measure they are right, for there is clearly a manifestation of two distinct phases of mental activity. But if such students will consider these "dual minds" in the light of the Hermetic Teachings regarding Vibrations and Mental Gender, they will see that the long sought for key is at hand.

In the phenomena of Telepathy it is seen how the Vibratory Energy of the Masculine Principle is projected toward the Feminine Principle of another person, and the latter takes the seed-thought and allows it to develop into maturity. In the same way Suggestion and Hypnotism operates. The Masculine Principle of the person giving the suggestions directs a stream of Vibratory Energy or Will-Power toward the Feminine Principle of the other person, and the latter accepting it makes it its own and acts and thinks accordingly. An idea thus lodged in the mind of another person grows and develops, and in time is regarded as the rightful mental offspring of the individual, whereas it is in reality like the cuckoo egg placed in the sparrows nest, where it destroys the rightful offspring and makes itself at home. The normal method is for the Masculine and Feminine Principles in a person's mind to co-ordinate and act harmoniously in conjunction with each other, but, unfortunately, the Masculine Principle in the average person is too lazy to act-the display of Will-Power is too slight-and the consequence is that such persons are ruled almost entirely by the minds and wills of other persons, whom they allow to do their thinking and willing for them. How few original thoughts or original actions are performed by the average person? Are not the majority of persons mere shadows and echoes of others having stronger wills or minds than themselves? The trouble is that the average person dwells almost altogether in his "Me" consciousness and does not realize that he has such a thing as an "I." He is polarized in his Feminine Principle of Mind, and the Masculine Principle, in which is lodged the Will, is allowed to remain inactive and not employed.

The strong men and women of the world invariably manifest the Masculine Principle of Will, and their strength depends materially upon this fact. Instead of living upon the impressions made upon their minds by others, they dominate their own minds by their Will, obtaining the kind of mental images desired, and moreover dominate the minds of others likewise, in the same manner. Look at the strong people, how they manage to implant their seed-thoughts in the minds of the masses of the people, thus causing the latter to think thoughts in accordance with the desires and wills of the strong individuals. This is why the masses of people are such sheeplike creatures, never originating an idea of their own, nor using their own powers of mental activity.

The manifestation of Mental Gender may be noticed all around us in everyday life. The magnetic persons are those who are able to use the Masculine Principle in the way of impressing their ideas upon others. The actor who makes people weep or cry as he wills, is employing this principle. And so is the successful orator, statesman, preacher, writer or other people who are before the public attention. The peculiar influence exerted by some people over others is due to the manifestation of Mental Gender, along the Vibrational lines above indicated. In this principle lies the secret of personal magnetism, personal influence, fascination, etc., as well as the phenomena generally grouped under the name of Hypnotism.

The student who has familiarized himself with the phenomena generally spoken of as "psychic" will have discovered the important part played in the said phenomena by that force which science has styled "Suggestion," by which term is meant the process or method whereby an idea is transferred to, or "impressed upon" the mind of another, causing the second mind to act in accordance therewith. A correct understanding of Suggestion is necessary in order to intelligently comprehend the varied psychical phenomena which Suggestion underlies. But, still more is a knowledge of Vibration and Mental Gender necessary for the student of Suggestion. For the whole principle of Suggestion depends upon the principle of Mental Gender and Vibration.

It is customary for the writers and teachers of Suggestion to explain that it is the "objective or voluntary" mind which make the mental impression, or suggestion, upon the "subjective or involuntary" mind. But they do not describe the process or give us any analogy in nature whereby we may more readily comprehend the idea. But if you will think of the matter in the light of the Hermetic Teachings you will be able to see that the energizing of the Feminine Principle by the Vibratory Energy of the Masculine Principle Is in accordance to the universal laws of nature, and that the natural world affords countless analogies whereby the principle may be understood. In fact, the Hermetic Teachings show that the very creation of the Universe follows the same law, and that in all creative manifestations, upon the planes of the spiritual, the mental, and the physical, there is always in operation this principle of Gender-this manifestation of the Masculine and the Feminine Principles. "As above, so below; as below, so above." And more than this, when the principle of Mental Gender is once grasped and understood, the varied phenomena of psychology at once becomes capable of intelligent classification and study, instead of being very much in the dark. The principle "works out" in practice, because it is based upon the immutable universal laws of life.

We shall not enter into an extended discussion of, or description of, the varied phenomena of mental influence or psychic activity. There are many books, many of them quite good, which have been written and published on this subject of late years. The main facts stated in these various books are correct, although the several writers have attempted to explain the phenomena by various pet theories of their own. The student may acquaint himself with these matters, and by using the theory of Mental Gender he will be able to bring order out of the chaos of conflicting theory and teachings, and may, moreover, readily make himself a master of the subject if he be so inclined. The purpose of this work is not to give an extended account of psychic phenomena but rather to give to the student a master-key whereby He may unlock the many doors leading into the parts of the Temple of Knowledge which he may wish to explore. We feel that in this consideration of the teachings of The Kybalion, one may find an explanation which will serve to clear away many perplexing difficulties—a key that will unlock many doors. What is the use of going into detail regarding all of the many features of psychic phenomena and mental science, provided we place in the hands of the student the means whereby he may acquaint himself fully regarding any phase of the subject which may interest him. With the aid of The Kybalion one may go through any occult library anew, the old

Light from Egypt illuminating many dark pages, and obscure subjects. That is the purpose of this book. We do not come expounding a new philosophy, but rather furnishing the outlines of a great world-old teaching which will make clear the teachings of others–which will serve as a Great Reconciler of differing: theories, and opposing doctrines.

ANNOTATIONS AND THOUGHTS OF THE KYBALION

About Hermes Trigistus

Hermes Trismegistus was an ancient Egyptian priest and philosopher who is credited with the invention of geometry, astronomy, and other sciences. He is also said to be the author of sacred texts that include The Emerald Tablet and The Corpus Hermeticum. Few people know about Hermes Trismegistus today or even understand his real identity.

He was known for being the founder of Hermeticism, which is a branch of esoteric philosophy. He lived from about the third century BC to about the second century AD. He was a phenomenal chemist and astrologer. He also wrote about various magical herbs, which he used in his work.

The life of Hermes Trismegistus was very mysterious. Even today, we don't know all the details about his life. What we do know is that he traveled extensively, and he spent a significant amount of time in Egypt. He also visited Syria, Greece, and Rome. We don't know what he did during his travels, but he must have made some incredible discoveries.

He also was a prolific author. He wrote about a variety of topics, including philosophy, alchemy, and magic. In addition, he is also responsible for developing the symbol of the hermetic cross. His work has had a significant impact on occult practices and philosophy.

Hermes Trismegistus was a remarkable individual who made significant contributions to occult philosophy and practices. His work has had a major impact on the development of modern occultism. If you're interested in learning more about him, I recommend reading any of his books or attending one of his lectures.

The importance of the Hermetica book.

The Hermetica book is a text written in Greek by the pseudonymous philosopher and scientist Hermes Trismegistus. It was composed between c. 150 BC and 50 AD, during the Hellenistic period of ancient Greece. The work consists of fourteen treatises on various esoteric topics, most notably alchemy and astrology.

Some people often consider it as a riddle book because of its symbols and esoteric teachings. It was written in the 14th century by Hermes Trismegistus. The book was important to Renaissance artists and philosophers because it provided them with a way to understand, interpret, and use symbolism. The book also had a a big influence on later thinkers, including Leonardo da Vinci and Galileo Galilei.

The Hermetica book was important to Renaissance artists and philosophers because it helped them to better understand the nature of symbols. They were able to see symbols in a new light and use them to convey mysterious messages. This was especially important to the Renaissance philosophers because they were interested in seeking knowledge beyond the normal everyday world.

THE BOOK ALSO HAD A BIG INFLUENCE ON LATER THINKERS because it helped them to understand the nature of symbols. They were also able to use them to convey messages that were hidden within the book. This allows for a deeper level of understanding and makes it easier for people to access knowledge that is otherwise difficult to find.

IT IS CONSIDERED AS A BIG SOURCE OF KNOWLEDGE THAT CAN be used to help people access information that is otherwise difficult to find. It was important to the Renaissance artists and philosophers because it allowed them to better understand the nature of symbols. This was especially important to the philosophers because they were interested in seeking knowledge beyond the normal everyday world.

SYMBOLS AND ITS MEANING INSIDE THE KYBALION BOOK

A SYMBOL IS A WORD, PICTURE, OR OTHER REPRESENTATION that stands for something else. Symbols can have positive or negative effects on people depending on how they are used. Some symbols have been around for thousands of years while others only became popular in the past few decades. The Kybalion book contains a variety of different symbols and their meanings. This article provides an overview of some common symbols found within the Kybalion book and discusses their possible implications.

THE KYBALION BOOK IS A BOOK ABOUT SYMBOLS. THE author, Dr. Johnurry, explains how different symbols have meaning and how you can use these symbols to improve your life. For example, the symbol for energy is a serpent eating its own tail. Dr. Johnurry explains that this symbol represents an endless cycle of energy which allows you to reach your goals. The symbol for intelligence is an eye. Dr. Johnurry explains that this symbol represents knowledge and understanding. There are also other symbols in the book including the symbol for balance, the symbol for truth, and the symbol for harmony.

HE ALSO THINKS THAT EACH SYMBOL HAS A SPECIFIC MEANING. For example, the symbol for energy represents the ability to reach your goals. The symbol for intelligence represents knowledge and understanding. The symbol for balance represents the ability to maintain equilibrium and control your emotions. The symbol for truth represents the ability to see things as they are. The symbol for harmony represents the ability to achieve balance in your life.

Dr. J explains that you can use symbols to improve your life by using these symbols to achieve specific goals. For example, you can use the symbol for energy to achieve your goals. You can use the symbol for intelligence to understand and learn new information. You can use the symbol for balance to maintain equilibrium and control your emotions. You can use the symbol for truth to see things as they are. You can also use the symbol for harmony to achieve balance in your life.

Seven Hermetic principles of The Kybalion explained

Many Hermetic principles have been identified within it, but seven are particularly relevant to this essay: 1) The Principle Of Vibration – This principle states that everything in existence is constantly oscillating between two extremes or poles. 2) The Principle Of Polarity – This says that every thing possesses a positive (energetic) as well as negative side. 3) The Principle Of

Rhythm – All things exist according as they follow certain rhythms or cycles.

THE BOOK IS A MODERN INTERPRETATION OF THE HERMETIC principles. It is a book that provides a comprehensive guide to understanding the universe and human life. The book is divided into seven chapters, each of which deals with a specific principle of the Hermetic philosophy.

THE FIRST PRINCIPLE OF THE KYBALION IS THE PRINCIPLE OF Polarity. This principle states that everything in the universe is dualistic – that there is a positive and negative aspect to everything. This principle is used to explain the existence of light and darkness, good and evil, and the way in which these two elements interact with each other.

THE SECOND PRINCIPLE OF THE KYBALION IS THE PRINCIPLE of Rhythm. This principle states that everything in the universe is subject to the laws of rhythm – that is, everything has a pattern, and this pattern is governed bylaws of rhythm. This principle is used to explain how things change over time, how chaos can be transformed into order, and how the order of the universe can be learned.

THE THIRD PRINCIPLE OF THE KYBALION IS THE PRINCIPLE OF Cause and Effect. This principle states that everything in the universe has a cause, and that this cause is always working towards a particular end. This principle is used to explain the way in which events in the universe are linked together, and the way in which change can happen.

THE FOURTH PRINCIPLE OF THE KYBALION IS THE PRINCIPLE of Correspondence. This principle states that everything in the universe is in perfect harmony with everything else. This principle is used to explain the way in which various elements of the universe work together, and the way in which elements of the universe can be combined to create new things.

THE FIFTH PRINCIPLE OF THE KYBALION IS THE PRINCIPLE OF Vibration. This principle states that everything in the universe is in a state of constant vibration. This principle is used to explain the way in which things move, and the way in which things change over time.

THE FINAL PRINCIPLE OF THE KYBALION IS THE PRINCIPLE OF analogy. This principle states that everything in the universe is based on analogy – that is, everything is based on relationships that can be observed between different things. This principle is used to explain the way in which things in the universe are similar to each other, and the way in which things in the universe are different from each other.

MEANING OF THE KYBALION BOOK

THE WORD "*KYBALION*" MEANS "CUBE OF LIFE." THE manuscript is purported to contain all of the most ancient teachings known to humanity. One of the central tenants of the Kybalion is the principle of first impression. The idea is that if you want something to have a positive effect on your life, you must first establish a good first impression. In other words, if you want to achieve success in any area of your life, you must begin by acting with integrity and exhibiting good character. Once you've built a good reputation and gained the trust of others, it becomes much easier to achieve your goals.

THE BOOK IS ALSO PACKED WITH INFORMATION ON SPIRITUAL helpers and guides, and it provides guidelines for developing and working with these powerful allies. It teaches that it is not enough to rely on the help of external forces to achieve our goals, we must also strive to create our own inner supports. Also discusses the importance of rhythm and music in the spiritual realm, and it offers tips for optimizing our energy and using it to achieve our goals.

NO MATTER WHAT YOUR GOALS MAY BE, THE KYBALION BOOK can help you achieve them. If you're looking for a resource that will help you tap into your inner power and potential, the Kybalion is the book for you.

The book is a valuable resource that can help you achieve your goals in life. Its teachings on first impression and spiritual helpers are particularly applicable to today's society, and its teachings on energy and rhythm are valuable tools for achieving success.

15

HERMETIC AXIOMS

"The possession of Knowledge, unless accompanied by a manifestation and expression in Action, is like the hoarding of precious metals—a vain and foolish thing. Knowledge, like wealth, is intended for Use. The Law of Use is Universal, and he who violates it suffers by reason of his conflict with natural forces."

— THE KYBALION.

The Hermetic Teachings, while always having been kept securely locked up in the minds of the fortunate possessors thereof, for reasons which we have already stated, were never intended to be merely stored away and secreted. The Law of Use is dwelt upon in the Teachings, as you may see by reference to the above quotation from The Kybalion, which states it forcibly. Knowledge without Use and Expression is a vain thing, bringing no good to its possessor, or to the race. Beware of Mental Miserliness, and express into Action that which you have learned. Study the Axioms and Aphorisms, but practice them also.

We give below some of the more important Hermetic Axioms, from The Kybalion, with a few comments added to each. Make these your own, and practice and use them, for they are not really your own until you have

Used them.

> *"To change your mood or mental state—change your vibration."*

One may change his mental vibrations by an effort of Will, in the direction of deliberately fixing the Attention upon a more desirable state. Will directs the Attention, and Attention changes the Vibration. Cultivate the Art of Attention, by means of the Will, and you have solved the secret of the Mastery of Moods and Mental States.

> *"To destroy an undesirable rate of mental vibration, put into operation the principle of Polarity and concentrate upon the opposite pole to that which you desire to suppress. Kill out the undesirable by changing its polarity."*

This is one of the most important of the Hermetic Formulas. It is based upon true scientific principles. We have shown you that a mental state and its opposite were merely the two poles of one thing, and that by Mental Transmutation the polarity might be reversed. This Principle is known to modern psychologists, who apply it to the breaking up of undesirable habits by bidding their students concentrate upon the opposite quality. If you are possessed of Fear, do not waste time trying to "kill out" Fear, but instead cultivate the quality of Courage, and the Fear will disappear. Some writers have expressed this idea most forcibly by using the illustration of the dark room. You do not have to shovel out or sweep out the Darkness, but by merely opening the shutters and letting in the Light the Darkness has disappeared. To kill out a Negative quality, concentrate upon the Positive Pole of that same quality, and the vibrations will gradually change from Negative to Positive, until finally you will become polarized on the Positive pole instead of the Negative. The reverse is also true, as many have found out to their sorrow, when they have allowed themselves to vibrate too constantly on the Negative pole of things. By changing your polarity you may master your moods, change your mental states, remake your disposition, and build up character. Much of the Mental Mastery of the advanced Hermetics is due to this application of Polarity, which is one of the important aspects of Mental Transmutation. Remember the Hermetic Axiom (quoted previously), which says:

> *"Mind (as well as metals and elements) may be transmuted from state to state; degree to degree, condition to condition; pole to pole; vibration to vibration."*

The mastery of Polarization is the mastery of the fundamental principles of Mental Transmutation or Mental Alchemy, for unless one acquires the art of changing his own polarity, he will be unable to affect his environment. An understanding of this principle will enable one to change his own Polarity, as well as that of others, if he will but devote the time, care, study and practice necessary to master the art. The principle is true, but the results obtained depend upon the persistent patience and practice of the student.

> *"Rhythm may be neutralized by an application of the Art of Polarization."*

As we have explained in previous chapters, the Hermetists hold that the Principle of Rhythm manifests on the Mental Plane as well as on the Physical Plane, and that the bewildering succession of moods, feelings, emotions, and other mental states, are due to the backward and forward swing of the mental pendulum, which carries us from one extreme of feeling to the other. The Hermetists also teach that the Law of Neutralization enables one, to a great extent, to overcome the operation of Rhythm in consciousness. As we have explained, there is a Higher Plane of Consciousness, as well as the ordinary Lower Plane, and the Master by rising mentally to the Higher Plane causes the swing of the mental pendulum to manifest on the Lower Plane, and he, dwelling on his Higher Plane, escapes the consciousness of the swing backward. This is effected by polarizing on the Higher Self, and thus raising the mental vibrations of the Ego above those of the ordinary plane of consciousness. It is akin to rising above a thing and allowing it to pass beneath you. The advanced Hermetist polarizes himself at the Positive Pole of his Being-the "I Am" pole rather than the pole of personality and by "refusing" and "denying" the operation of Rhythm, raises himself above its plane of consciousness, and standing firm in his Statement of Being he allows the pendulum to swing back on the Lower Plane without changing his Polarity. This is accomplished by all individuals who have attained any degree of self-mastery, whether they understand the law or not. Such persons simply "refuse" to allow themselves to be swung back by the pendulum of mood and emotion, and by steadfastly affirming the superiority they remain polarized on the Positive pole. The Master, of course, attains a far greater degree of proficiency, because he understands the law which he is overcoming by a higher law, and by the use of his Will he attains a degree of Poise and Mental Steadfastness almost impossible of belief on the part of those who allow themselves to be swung backward and forward by the mental pendulum of moods and feelings.

Remember always, however, that you do not really destroy the Principle of Rhythm, for that is indestructible. You simply overcome one law by counter-balancing it with another and thus maintain an equilibrium. The laws of balance and counterbalance are in operation on the mental as well as on the physical planes, and an understanding of these laws enables one to seem to overthrow laws, whereas he is merely exerting a counterbalance.

> *"Nothing escapes the Principle of Cause and Effect, but there are many Planes of Causation, and one may use the laws of the higher to overcome the laws of the lower."*

By an understanding of the practice of Polarization, the Hermetists rise to a higher plane of Causation and thus counterbalance the laws of the lower planes of Causation. By rising above the plane of ordinary Causes they become themselves, in a degree, Causes instead of being merely Caused. By being able to master their own moods and feelings, and by being able to neutralize Rhythm, as we have already explained, they are able to escape a great part of the operations of Cause and Effect on the ordinary plane. The masses of people are carried along, obedient to their environment; the wills and desires of others stronger than themselves; the effects of inherited tendencies; the suggestions of those about them; and other outward causes; which tend to move them about on the chess-board of life like mere pawns. By rising above these influencing causes, the advanced Hermetists seek a higher plane of mental action, and by dominating their moods, emotions, impulses and feelings, they create for themselves new characters, qualities and powers, by which they overcome their ordinary environment, and thus become practically players instead of mere Pawns. Such people help to play the game of life understandingly, instead of being moved about this way and that way by stronger influences and powers and wills. They use the Principle of Cause and Effect, instead of being used by it. Of course, even the highest are subject to the Principle as it manifests on the higher planes, but on the lower planes of activity, they are Masters instead of Slaves. As The Kybalion says:

> *"The wise ones serve on the higher, but rule on the lower. They obey the laws coming from above them, But on their own plane, and those below them they rule and give orders. And, yet, in so doing, they form a part of the Principle, instead of opposing it. The wise man falls in with the Law, and by understanding its movements he operates it instead of being its blind slave. Just as does the skilled swimmer turn this way and that way, going and coming as he will, instead of being as the log which is carried here and there—so is the wise man as compared to the ordinary man—and yet both swimmer and log; wise man and fool, are subject to Law. He who understands this is well on the road to Mastery."*

In conclusion let us again call your attention to the Hermetic Axiom:

"True Hermetic Transmutation is a Mental Art."

In the above axiom, the Hermetists teach that the great work of influencing one's environment is accomplished by Mental Power.

The Universe being wholly mental, it follows that it may be ruled only by Mentality. And in this truth is to be found an explanation of all the phenomena and manifestations of the various mental powers which are attracting so much attention and study in these earlier years of the Twentieth Century. Back of and under the teachings of the various cults and schools, remains ever constant the Principle of the Mental Substance of the Universe. If the Universe be Mental in its substantial nature, then it follows that Mental Transmutation must change the conditions and phenomena of the Universe. If the Universe is Mental, then Mind must be the highest power affecting its phenomena. If this be understood then all the so-called "miracles" and "wonder-workings" are seen plainly for what they are.

"THE ALL is MIND; The Universe is Mental."

— THE KYBALION.

FINIS

THE CORPUS
HERMETICUM

I

POEMANDRES, THE SHEPHERD OF MEN

‹This is the most famous of the Hermetic documents, a revelation account describing a vision of the creation of the universe and the nature and fate of humanity. Authors from the Renaissance onward have been struck by the way in which its creation myth seems partly inspired by Genesis, partly reacting against it. The Fall has here become the descent of the Primal Man through the spheres of the planets to the world of Nature, a descent caused not by disobedience but by love, and done with the blessing of God.

‹The seven rulers of fate discussed in sections 9, 14 and 25 are the archons of the seven planets, which also appear in Plato's Timaeus and in a number of the ancient writings usually lumped together as "Gnostic". Their role here is an oddly ambivalent one, powers of Harmony who are nonetheless the sources of humanity's tendencies to evil. ›

1. It chanced once on a time my mind was meditating on the things that are, my thought was raised to a great height, the senses of my body being held back - just as men who are weighed down with sleep after a fill of food, or from fatigue of body.

Methought a Being more than vast, in size beyond all bounds, called out my name and saith: What wouldst thou hear and see, and what hast thou in mind to learn and know?

2. And I do say: Who art thou?

He saith: I am Man-Shepherd (Poemandres), Mind of all-masterhood; I know what thou desirest and I'm with thee everywhere.

3. [And] I reply: I long to learn the things that are, and comprehend their nature, and know God. This is, I said, what I desire to hear.

He answered back to me: Hold in thy mind all thou wouldst know, and I will teach thee.

4. E'en with these words His aspect changed, and straightway, in the twinkling of an eye, all things were opened to me, and I see a Vision limitless, all things turned into Light – sweet, joyous [Light]. And I became transported as I gazed.

But in a little while Darkness came settling down on part [of it], awesome and gloomy, coiling in sinuous folds, so that methought it like unto a snake.

And then the Darkness changed into some sort of a Moist Nature, tossed about beyond all power of words, belching out smoke as from a fire, and groaning forth a wailing sound that beggars all description.

[And] after that an outcry inarticulate came forth from it, as though it were a Voice of Fire.

5. [Thereon] out of the Light [...] a Holy Word (Logos) descended on that Nature. And upwards to the height from the Moist Nature leaped forth pure Fire; light was it, swift and active too.

The Air, too, being light, followed after the Fire; from out of the Earth-and-Water rising up to Fire so that it seemed to hang therefrom.

But Earth-and-Water stayed so mingled with each other, that Earth from Water no one could discern. Yet were they moved to hear by reason of the Spirit-Word (Logos) pervading them.

6. Then saith to me Man-Shepherd: Didst understand this Vision what it means?

Nay; that shall I know, said I.

That Light, He said, am I, thy God, Mind, prior to Moist Nature which appeared from Darkness; the Light-Word (Logos) [that appeared] from Mind is Son of God.

What then? - say I.

Know that what sees in thee and hears is the Lord's Word (Logos); but Mind is Father-God. Not separate are they the one from other; just in their union [rather] is it Life consists.

Thanks be to Thee, I said.

So, understand the Light [He answered], and make friends with it.

7. And speaking thus He gazed for long into my eyes, so that I trembled at the look of him.

But when He raised His head, I see in Mind the Light, [but] now in Powers no man could number, and Cosmos grown beyond all bounds, and that the Fire was compassed round about by a most mighty Power, and [now] subdued had come unto a stand.

And when I saw these things I understood by reason of Man-Shepherd's Word (Logos).

8. But as I was in great astonishment, He saith to me again: Thou didst behold in Mind the Archetypal Form whose being is before beginning without end. Thus spake to me Man-Shepherd.

And I say: Whence then have Nature's elements their being?

To this He answer gives: From Will of God. [Nature] received the Word (Logos), and gazing upon the Cosmos Beautiful did copy it, making herself into a cosmos, by means of her own elements and by the births of souls.

9. And God-the-Mind, being male and female both, as Light and Life subsisting, brought forth another Mind to give things form, who, God as he was of Fire and Spirit, formed Seven Rulers who enclose the cosmos that the sense perceives. Men call their ruling Fate.

10. Straightway from out the downward elements God's Reason (Logos) leaped up to Nature's pure formation, and was at-oned with the Formative Mind; for it was co-essential with it. And Nature's downward elements were thus left reason-less, so as to be pure matter.

11. Then the Formative Mind ([at-oned] with Reason), he who surrounds the spheres and spins them with his whorl, set turning his formations, and let them turn from a beginning boundless unto an endless end. For that the circulation of these [spheres] begins where it doth end, as Mind doth will.

And from the downward elements Nature brought forth lives reason-less; for He did not extend the Reason (Logos) [to them]. The Air brought forth things winged; the Water things that swim, and Earth-and-Water one from another parted, as Mind willed. And from her bosom Earth produced what lives she had, four-footed things and reptiles, beasts wild and tame.

12. But All-Father Mind, being Life and Light, did bring forth Man co-equal to Himself, with whom He fell in love, as being His own child; for he was beautiful beyond compare, the Image of his Sire. In very truth, God fell in love with his own Form; and on him did bestow all of His own formations.

13. And when he gazed upon what the Enformer had created in the Father, [Man] too wished to enform; and [so] assent was given him by the Father.

Changing his state to the formative sphere, in that he was to have his whole authority, he gazed upon his Brother's creatures. They fell in love with him, and gave him each a share of his own ordering.

And after that he had well learned their essence and had become a sharer in their nature, he had a mind to break right through the Boundary of their spheres, and to subdue the might of that which pressed upon the Fire.

14. So he who hath the whole authority o'er [all] the mortals in the cosmos and o'er its lives irrational, bent his face downwards through the Harmony, breaking right through its strength, and showed to downward Nature God's fair form.

And when she saw that Form of beauty which can never satiate, and him who [now] possessed within himself each single energy of [all seven] Rulers as well as God's own Form, she smiled with love; for 'twas as though she'd seen the image of Man's fairest form upon her Water, his shadow on her Earth.

He in turn beholding the form like to himself, existing in her, in her Water, loved it and willed to live in it; and with the will came act, and [so] he vivified the form devoid of reason.

And Nature took the object of her love and wound herself completely around him, and they were intermingled, for they were lovers.

15. And this is why beyond all creatures on the earth man is twofold; mortal because of body, but because of the essential man immortal.

Though deathless and possessed of sway o'er all, yet doth he suffer as a mortal doth, subject to Fate.

Thus though above the Harmony, within the Harmony he hath become a slave. Though male-female, as from a Father male-female, and though he's sleepless from a sleepless [Sire], yet is he overcome [by sleep].

16. Thereon [I say: Teach on], O Mind of me, for I myself as well am amorous of the Word (Logos).

The Shepherd said: This is the mystery kept hid until this day.

Nature embraced by Man brought forth a wonder, oh so wonderful. For as he had the nature of the Concord of the Seven, who, as I said to thee, [were made] of Fire and Spirit - Nature delayed not, but immediately brought forth seven "men", in correspondence with the natures of the Seven, male-female and moving in the air.

Thereon [I said]: O Shepherd, ..., for now I'm filled with great desire and long to hear; do not run off.

The Shepherd said: Keep silence, for not as yet have I unrolled for thee the first discourse (logoi).

Lo! I am still, I said.

17. In such wise than, as I have said, the generation of these seven came to pass. Earth was as woman, her Water filled with

longing; ripeness she took from Fire, spirit from Aether. Nature thus brought forth frames to suit the form of Man.

And Man from Light and Life changed into soul and mind – from Life to soul, from Light to mind.

And thus continued all the sense-world's parts until the period of their end and new beginnings.

18. Now listen to the rest of the discourse (Logos) which thou dost long to hear.

The period being ended, the bond that bound them all was loosened by God's Will. For all the animals being male-female, at the same time with Man were loosed apart; some became partly male, some in like fashion [partly] female. And straightway God spake by His Holy Word (Logos):

"Increase ye in increasing, and multiply in multitude, ye creatures and creations all; and man that hath Mind in him, let him learn to know that he himself is deathless, and that the cause of death is love, though Love is all."

19. When He said this, His Forethought did by means of Fate and Harmony effect their couplings and their generations founded. And so all things were multiplied according to their kind.

And he who thus hath learned to know himself, hath reached that Good which doth transcend abundance; but he who through a love that leads astray, expends his love upon his body – he stays in Darkness wandering, and suffering through his senses things of Death.

20. What is the so great fault, said I, the ignorant commit, that they should be deprived of deathlessness?

Thou seem'st, He said, O thou, not to have given heed to what thou heardest. Did I not bid thee think?

Yea do I think, and I remember, and therefore give Thee thanks.

If thou didst think [thereon], [said He], tell me: Why do they merit death who are in Death?

It is because the gloomy Darkness is the root and base of the material frame; from it came the Moist Nature; from this the body in the sense-world was composed; and from this [body] Death doth the Water drain.

21. Right was thy thought, O thou! But how doth "he who knows himself, go unto Him", as God's Word (Logos) hath declared?

And I reply: the Father of the universals doth consist of Light and Life, from Him Man was born.

Thou sayest well, [thus] speaking. Light and Life is Father-God, and from Him Man was born.

If then thou learnest that thou art thyself of Life and Light, and that thou [happen'st] to be out of them, thou shalt return again to Life. Thus did Man-Shepherd speak.

But tell me further, Mind of me, I cried, how shall I come to Life again...for God doth say: "The man who hath Mind in him, let him learn to know that he himself [is deathless]."

22. Have not all men then Mind?

Thou sayest well, O thou, thus speaking. I, Mind, myself am present with holy men and good, the pure and merciful, men who live piously.

[To such] my presence doth become an aid, and straightway they gain gnosis of all things, and win the Father's love by their pure lives, and give Him thanks, invoking on Him blessings, and chanting hymns, intent on Him with ardent love.

And ere they give up the body unto its proper death, they turn them with disgust from its sensations, from knowledge of what things they operate. Nay, it is I, the Mind, that will not let the operations which befall the body, work to their [natural] end. For being door-keeper I'll close up [all] the entrances, and cut the mental actions off which base and evil energies induce.

23. But to the Mind-less ones, the wicked and depraved, the envious and covetous, and those who mured do and love impiety, I am far off, yielding my place to the Avenging Daimon, who sharpening the fire, tormenteth him and addeth fire to fire upon him, and rusheth upon him through his senses, thus rendering him readier for transgressions of the law, so that he meets with greater torment; nor doth he ever cease to have desire for appetites inordinate, insatiately striving in the dark.

24. Well hast thou taught me all, as I desired, O Mind. And now, pray, tell me further of the nature of the Way Above as now it is [for me].

To this Man-Shepherd said: When the material body is to be dissolved, first thou surrenderest the body by itself unto the work of change, and thus the form thou hadst doth vanish, and thou surrenderest thy way of life, void of its energy, unto the Daimon. The body's senses next pass back into their sources, becoming separate, and resurrect as energies; and passion and desire withdraw unto that nature which is void of reason.

25. And thus it is that man doth speed his way thereafter upwards through the Harmony.

To the first zone he gives the Energy of Growth and Waning; unto the second [zone], Device of Evils [now] de-energized; unto the third, the Guile of the Desires de-energized; unto the fourth, his Domineering Arrogance, [also] de-energized; unto the fifth, unholy Daring and the Rashness of Audacity, de-energized; unto the sixth, Striving for Wealth by evil means, deprived of its aggrandizement; and to the seventh zone, Ensnaring Falsehood, de-energized.

26. And then, with all the energisings of the harmony stript from him, clothed in his proper Power, he cometh to that Nature which belongs unto the Eighth, and there with those-that-are hymneth the Father.

They who are there welcome his coming there with joy; and he, made like to them that sojourn there, doth further hear the Powers who are above the Nature that belongs unto the Eighth, singing their songs of praise to God in language of their own.

And then they, in a band, go to the Father home; of their own selves they make surrender of themselves to Powers, and [thus] becoming Powers they are in God. This the good end for those who have gained Gnosis - to be made one with God.

Why shouldst thou then delay? Must it not be, since thou hast all received, that thou shouldst to the worthy point the way, in order that through thee the race of mortal kind may by [thy] God be saved?

27. This when He'd said, Man-Shepherd mingled with the Powers.

But I, with thanks and belssings unto the Father of the universal [Powers], was freed, full of the power he had poured into me, and full of what He'd taught me of the nature of the All and of the loftiest Vision.

And I began to preach unto men the Beauty of Devotion and of Gnosis:

O ye people, earth-born folk, ye who have given yourselves to drunkenness and sleep and ignorance of God, be sober now, cease from your surfeit, cease to be glamoured by irrational sleep!

28. And when they heard, they came with one accord. Whereon I say:

Ye earth-born folk, why have ye given yourselves up to Death, while yet ye have the power of sharing Deathlessness? Repent, O ye, who walk with Error arm in arm and make of Ignorance the sharer of your board; get ye out from the light of Darkness, and take your part in Deathlessness, forsake Destruction!

29. And some of them with jests upon their lips departed [from me], abandoning themselves unto the Way of Death; others entreated to be taught, casting themselves before my feet.

But I made them arise, and I became a leader of the Race towards home, teaching the words (logoi), how and in what way they shall be saved. I sowed in them the words (logoi) of wisdom; of Deathless Water were they given to drink.

And when even was come and all sun's beams began to set, I bade them all give thanks to God. And when they had brought to an end the giving of their thanks, each man returned to his own resting place.

30. But I recorded in my heart Man-Shepherd's benefaction, and with my every hope fulfilled more than rejoiced. For body's sleep became the soul's awakening, and closing of the eyes - true vision, pregnant with Good my silence, and the utterance of my word (logos) begetting of good things.

All this befell me from my Mind, that is Man-Shepherd, Word (Logos) of all masterhood, by whom being God-inspired I came unto the Plain of Truth. Wherefore with all my soul and strength thanksgiving give I unto Father-God.

31. Holy art Thou, O God, the universals' Father.

Holy art Thou, O God, whose Will perfects itself by means of its own Powers.

Holy art Thou, O God, who willeth to be known and art known by Thine own.

Holy art Thou, who didst by Word (Logos) make to consist the things that are.

Holy art Thou, of whom All-nature hath been made an image.

Holy art Thou, whose Form Nature hath never made.

Holy art Thou, more powerful than all power.

Holy art Thou, transcending all pre-eminence.

Holy Thou art, Thou better than all praise.

Accept my reason's offerings pure, from soul and heart for aye stretched up to Thee, O Thou unutterable, unspeakable, Whose Name naught but the Silence can express.

32. Give ear to me who pray that I may ne'er of Gnosis fail, [Gnosis] which is our common being's nature; and fill me with Thy Power, and with this Grace [of Thine], that I may give the Light to those in ignorance of the Race, my Brethren, and Thy Sons.

For this cause I believe, and I bear witness; I go to Life and Light. Blessed art Thou, O Father. Thy Man would holy be as Thou art holy, e'en as Thou gave him Thy full authority [to be].

2
TO ASCLEPIUS

<This dialogue sets forth the difference between the physical and metaphysical worlds in the context of Greek natural philosophy. Some of the language is fairly technical: the "errant spheres" of sections 6 and 7 are the celestial spheres carrying the planets, while the "inerrant sphere" is that of the fixed stars. It's useful to keep in mind, also, that "air" and "spirit" are interchangeable concepts in Greek thought, and that the concept of the Good has a range of implications which don't come across in the English word: one is that the good of any being, in Greek thought, was also that being's necessary goal.

<The criticism of childlessness in section 17 should probably be read as a response to the Christian ideal of celibacy, which horrified many people in the ancient world. >

1. Hermes: All that is moved, Asclepius, is it not moved in something and by something?

Asclepius: Assuredly.

H: And must not that in which it's moved be greater than the moved?

A: It must.

H: Mover, again, has greater power than moved?

A: It has, of course.

H: The nature, furthermore, of that in which it's moved must be quite other from the nature of the moved?

A: It must completely.

2. H: Is not, again, this cosmos vast, [so vast] that than it there exists no body greater?

A: Assuredly.

H: And massive, too, for it is crammed with multitudes of other mighty frames, nay, rather all the other bodies that there are?

A: It is.

H: And yet the cosmos is a body?

A: It is a body.

H: And one that's moved?

3. A: Assuredly.

H: Of what size, then, must be the space in which it's moved, and of what kind [must be] the nature [of that space]? Must it not be far vaster [than the cosmos], in order that it may be able to find room for its continued course, so that the moved may not be cramped for want of room and lose its motion?

A: Something, Thrice-greatest one, it needs must be, immensely vast.

4. H: And of what nature? Must it not be, Asclepius, of just the contrary? And is not contrary to body bodiless?

A: Agreed.

H: Space, then, is bodiless. But bodiless must either be some godlike thing or God [Himself]. And by "some godlike thing" I mean no more the generable [i.e., that which is generated] but the ingenerable.

5. If, then, space be some godlike thing, it is substantial; but if 'tis God [Himself], it transcends substance. But it is to be thought of otherwise [than God], and in this way.

God is first "thinkable" <or "intelligible"> for us, not for Himself, for that the thing that's thought doth fall beneath the thinker's sense. God then cannot be "thinkable" unto Himself, in that He's thought of by Himself as being nothing else but what He thinks. But he is "something else" for us, and so He's thought of by us.

6. If space is, therefore, to be thought, [it should] not, [then, be thought as] God, but space. If God is also to be thought, [He should] not [be conceived] as space, but as energy that can contain [all space].

Further, all that is moved is moved not in the moved but in the stable. And that which moves [another] is of course stationary, for 'tis impossible that it should move with it.

A: How is it, then, that things down here, Thrice-greatest one, are moved with those that are [already] moved? For thou hast said the errant spheres were moved by the inerrant one.

H: This is not, O Asclepius, a moving with, but one against; they are not moved with one another, but one against the other. It is this contrariety which turneth the resistance of their motion into rest. For that resistance is the rest of motion.

7. Hence, too, the errant spheres, being moved contrarily to the inerrant one, are moved by one another by mutual contrariety, [and also] by the spable one through contrariety itself. And this can otherwise not be.

The Bears up there <i.e., Ursa Major and Minor>, which neither set nor rise, think'st thou they rest or move?

A: They move, Thrice-greatest one.

H: And what their motion, my Asclepius?

A: Motion that turns for ever round the same.

H: But revolution - motion around same - is fixed by rest. For "round-the-same" doth stop "beyond-same". "Beyond-same" then, being stopped, if it be steadied in "round-same" - the contrary stands firm, being rendered ever stable by its contrariety.

8. Of this I'll give thee here on earth an instance, which the eye can see. Regard the animals down here - a man, for instance, swimming! The water moves, yet the resistance of his hands and feet give him stability, so that he is not borne along with it, nor sunk thereby.

A: Thou hast, Thrice-greatest one, adduced a most clear instance.

H: All motion, then, is caused in station and by station.

The motion, therefore, of the cosmos (and of every other hylic <i.e., material> animal) will not be caused by things exterior to the cosmos, but by things interior [outward] to the exterior -

such [things] as soul, or spirit, or some such other thing incorporeal.

'Tis not the body that doth move the living thing in it; nay, not even the whole [body of the universe a lesser] body e'en though there be no life in it.

9. A: What meanest thou by this, Thrice-greatest one? Is it not bodies, then, that move the stock and stone and all the other things inanimate?

H: By no means, O Asclepius. The something-in-the-body, the that-which-moves the thing inanimate, this surely's not a body, for that it moves the two of them - both body of the lifter and the lifted? So that a thing that's lifeless will not move a lifeless thing. That which doth move [another thing] is animate, in that it is the mover.

Thou seest, then, how heavy laden is the soul, for it alone doth lift two bodies. That things, moreover, moved are moved in something as well as moved by something is clear.

10. A: Yea, O Thrice-greatest one, things moved must needs be moved in something void.

H: Thou sayest well, O [my] Asclepius! For naught of things that are is void. Alone the "is-not" is void [and] stranger to subsistence. For that which is subsistent can never change to void.

A: Are there, then, O Thrice-greatest one, no such things as an empty cask, for instance, and an empty jar, a cup and vat, and other things like unto them?

H: Alack, Asclepius, for thy far-wandering from the truth! Think'st thou that things most full and most replete are void?

11. A: How meanest thou, Thrice-greatest one?

H: Is not air body?

A: It is.

H: And doth this body not pervade all things, and so, pervading, fill them? And "body"; doth body not consist from blending of the "four" <elements>? Full, then, of air are all thou callest void; and if of air, then of the "four".

Further, of this the converse follows, that all thou callest full are void - of air; for that they have their space filled out with other bodies, and, therefore, are not able to receive the air therein. These, then, which thou dost say are void, they should be hollow named, not void; for they not only are, but they are full of air and spirit.

12. A: Thy argument (logos), Thrice-greatest one, is not to be gainsaid; air is a body. Further, it is this body which doth pervade all things, and so, pervading, fill them. What are we, then, to call that space in which the all doth move?

H: The bodiless, Asclepius.

A: What, then, is Bodiless?

H: 'Tis Mind and Reason (logos), whole out of whole, all self-embracing, free from all body, from all error free, unsensible to body and untouchable, self stayed in self, containing all, preserving those that are, whose rays, to use a likeness, are Good, Truth, Light beyond light, the Archetype of soul.

A: What, then, is God?

13. H: Not any one of these is He; for He it is that causeth them to be, both all and each and every thing of all that are. Nor hath He left a thing beside that is-not; but they are all from things-that-are and not from things-that-are-not. For that the things-

that-are-not have naturally no power of being anything, but naturally have the power of the inability-to-be. And, conversely, the things-that-are have not the nature of some time not-being.

14. A: What say'st thou ever, then, God is?

H: God, therefore, is not Mind, but Cause that the Mind is; God is not Spirit, but Cause that Spirit is; God is not Light, but Cause that the Light is. Hence one should honor God with these two names [the Good and Father] - names which pertain to Him alone and no one else.

For no one of the other so-called gods, no one of men, or daimones, can be in any measure Good, but God alone; and He is Good alone and nothing else. The rest of things are separable all from the Good's nature; for [all the rest] are soul and body, which have no place that can contain the Good.

15. For that as mighty is the Greatness of the Good as is the Being of all things that are - both bodies and things bodiless, things sensible and intelligible things. Call thou not, therefore, aught else Good, for thou would'st imious be; nor anything at all at any time call God but Good alone, for so thou would'st again be impious.

16. Though, then, the Good is spoken of by all, it is not understood by all, what thing it is. Not only, then, is God not understood by all, but both unto the gods and some of the men they out of ignorance do give the name of Good, though they can never either be or become Good. For they are very different from God, while Good can never be distinguished from Him, for that God is the same as Good.

The rest of the immortal ones are nonetheless honored with the name of God, and spoken of as gods; but God is Good not out of courtesy but out of nature. For that God's nature and the

Good is one; one os the kind of both, from which all other kinds [proceed].

The Good is he who gives all things and naught receives. God, then, doth give all things and receive naught. God, then, is Good, and Good is God.

17. The other name of God is Father, again because He is the that-which-maketh-all. The part of father is to make.

Wherefore child-making is a very great and a most pious thing in life for them who think aright, and to leave life on earth without a child a very great misfortune and impiety; and he who hath no child is punished by the daimones after death.

And this is the punishment: that that man's soul who hath no child, shall be condemned unto a body with neither man's nor woman's nature, a thing accursed beneath the sun.

Wherefore, Asclepius, let not your sympathies be with the man who hath no child, but rather pity his mishap, knowing what punishment abides for him.

Let all that has been said then, be to thee, Asclepius, an introduction to the gnosis of the nature of all things.

3
THE SACRED SERMON

<This brief and apparently somewhat garbled text recounts the creation and nature of the world in terms much like those of the Poemandres. The major theme is the renewal of all things in a cyclic universe, with the seven planetary rulers again playing a major role. >

1. The Glory of all things is God, Godhead and Godly Nature. Source of the things that are is God, who is both Mind and Nature - yea Matter, the Wisdom that reveals all things. Source [too] is Godhead - yea Nature, Energy, Necessity, and End, and Making-new-again.

Darkness that knew no bounds was in Abyss, and Water [too] and subtle Breath intelligent; these were by Power of God in Chaos.

Then Holy Light arose; and there collected 'neath Dry Space <literally: "sand"> from out Moist Essence Elements; and all the Gods do separate things out from fecund Nature.

2. All things being undefined and yet unwrought, the light things were assigned unto the height, the heavy ones had their foundations laid down underneath the moist part of Dry Space, the universal things being bounded off by Fire and hanged in Breath to keep them up.

And Heaven was seen in seven circles; its Gods were visible in forms of stars with all their signs; while Nature had her members made articulate together with the Gods in her. And [Heaven's] periphery revolved in cyclic course, borne on by Breath of God.

3. And every God by his own proper power brought forth what was appointed him. Thus there arose four-footed beasts, and creeping things, and those that in the water dwell, and things with wings, and everything that beareth seed, and grass, and shoot of every flower, all having in themselves seed of again-becoming.

And they selected out the births of men for gnosis of the works of God and attestation of the energy of Nature; the multitude of men for lordship over all beneath the heaven and gnosis of its blessings, that they might increase in increasing and multiply in multitude, and every soul infleshed by revolution of the Cyclic Gods, for observation of the marvels of Heaven and Heaven's Gods' revolution, and of the works of God and energy of Nature, for tokens of its blessings, for gnosis of the power of God, that they might know the fates that follow good and evil [deeds] and learn the cunning work of all good arts.

4. [Thus] there begins their living and their growing wise, according to the fate appointed by the revolution of the Cyclic Gods, and their deceasing for this end.

And there shall be memorials mighty of their handiworks upon the earth, leaving dim trace behind when cycles are renewed.

For every birth of flesh ensouled, and of the fruit of seed, and every handiwork, though it decay, shall of necessity renew itself, both by the renovation of the Gods and by the turning-round of Nature's rhythmic wheel.

4
THE CUP OR MONAD

<This short text gives an unusually lucid overview of the foundations of Hermetic thought. The stress on rejection of the body and its pleasures, and on the division of humanity into those with Mind and those without, are reminiscent of some of the so-called "Gnostic" writings of the same period. The idea that the division is a matter of choice, on the other hand, is a pleasant variation on the almost Calvinist flavor of writings such as the Apocalypse of Adam.

<Mead speculates that the imagery of the Cup in this text may have a distant connection, by way of unorthodox ideas about Communion, with the legends of the Holy Grail. >

1. Hermes: With Reason (Logos), not with hands, did the World-maker make the universal World; so that thou shouldst think of him as everywhere and ever-being, the Author of all things, and One and Only, who by His Will all beings hath created.

This Body of Him is a thing no man can touch, or see, or measure, a body inextensible, like to no other frame. 'Tis neither

Fire nor Water, Air nor Breath; yet all of them come from it. Now being Good he willed to consecrate this [Body] to Himself alone, and set its Earth in order and adorn it.

2. So down [to Earth] He sent the Cosmos of this Frame Divine – man, a life that cannot die, and yet a life that dies. And o'er [all other] lives and over Cosmos [too], did man excel by reason of the Reason (Logos) and the Mind. For contemplator of God's works did man become; he marvelled and did strive to know their Author.

3. Reason (Logos) indeed, O Tat, among all men hath He distributed, but Mind not yet; not that He grudgeth any, for grudging cometh not from Him, but hath its place below, within the souls of men who have no Mind.

Tat: Why then did God, O father, not on all bestow a share of Mind?

H: He willed, my son, to have it set up in the midst for souls, just as it were a prize.

4. T: And where hath He set it up?

H: He filled a mighty Cup with it, and sent it down, joining a Herald [to it], to whom He gave command to make this proclamation to the hearts of men:

Baptize thyself with this Cup's baptism, what heart can do so, thou that hast faith thou canst ascend to him that hath sent down the Cup, thou that dost know for what thoudidst come into being!

As many then as understood the Herald's tidings and doused themselves in Mind, became partakers in the Gnosis; and when they had "received the Mind" they were made "perfect men".

But they who do not understand the tidings, these, since they possess the aid of Reason [only] and not Mind, are ignorant wherefor they have come into being and whereby.

5. The senses of such men are like irrational creatures'; and as their [whole] make-up is in their feelings and their impulses, they fail in all appreciation of <lit.: "they do not wonder at"> those things which really are worth contemplation. These center all their thought upon the pleasures of the body and its appetites, in the belief that for its sake man hath come into being.

But they who have received some portion of God's gift, these, Tat, if we judge by their deeds, have from Death's bonds won their release; for they embrace in their own Mind all things, things on the earth, things in the heaven, and things above the heaven - if there be aught. And having raised themselves so far they sight the Good; and having sighted it, they look upon their sojourn here as a mischance; and in disdain of all, both things in body and the bodiless, they speed their way unto that One and Only One.

6. This is, O Tat, the Gnosis of the Mind, Vision of things Divine; God-knowledge is it, for the Cup is God's.

T: Father, I, too, would be baptized.

H: Unless thou first shall hate thy Body, son, thou canst not love thy Self. But if thou lov'st thy Self thou shalt have Mind, and having Mind thou shalt share in the Gnosis.

T: Father, what dost thou mean?

H: It is not possible, my son, to give thyself to both - I mean to things that perish and to things divine. For seeing that existing things are twain, Body and Bodiless, in which the perishing and the divine are understood, the man who hath the will to choose is left the choice of one or the other; for it can never be the twain should meet. And in those souls to whom the choice is left, the waning of the one causes the other's growth to show itself.

7. Now the choosing of the Better not only proves a lot most fair for him who makes the choice, seeing it makes the man a God, but also shows his piety to God. Whereas the [choosing] of the Worse, although it doth destroy the "man", it doth only disturb God's harmony to this extent, that as processions pass by in the middle of the way, without being able to do anything but take the road from others, so do such men move in procession through the world led by their bodies' pleasures.

8. This being so, O Tat, what comes from God hath been and will be ours; but that which is dependent on ourselves, let this press onward and have no delay, for 'tis not God, 'tis we who are the cause of evil things, preferring them to good.

Thou see'st, son, how many are the bodies through which we have to pass, how many are the choirs of daimones, how vast the system of the star-courses [through which our Path doth lie], to hasten to the One and Only God.

For to the Good there is no other shore; It hath no bounds; It is without an end; and for Itself It is without beginning, too, though unto us it seemeth to have one - the Gnosis.

9. Therefore to It Gnosis is no beginning; rather is it [that Gnosis doth afford] to us the first beginning of its being known.

Let us lay hold, therefore, of the beginning. and quickly speed through all [we have to pass].

'Tis very hard, to leave the things we have grown used to, which meet our gaze on every side, and turn ourselves back to the Old Old [Path].

Appearances delight us, whereas things which appear not make their believing hard.

Now evils are the more apparent things, whereas the Good can never show Itself unto the eyes, for It hath neither form nor figure.

Therefore the Good is like Itself alone, and unlike all things else; or 'tis impossible that That which hath no body should make Itself apparent to a body.

10. The "Like's" superiority to the "Unlike" and the "Unlike's" inferiority unto the "Like" consists in this:

The Oneness being Source and Root of all, is in all things as Root and Source. Without [this] Source is naught; whereas the Source [Itself] is from naught but itself, since it is Source of all the rest. It is Itself Its Source, since It may have no other Source.

The Oneness then being Source, containeth every number, but is contained by none; engendereth every number, but is engendered by no other one.

11. Now all that is engendered is imperfect, it is divisible, to increase subject and to decrease; but with the Perfect [One] none of these things doth hold. Now that which is increasable increases from the Oneness, but succumbs through its own feebleness when it no longer can contain the One.

And now, O Tat, God's Image hath been sketched for thee, as far as it can be; and if thou wilt attentively dwell on it and observe it with thine heart's eyes, believe me, son, thou'lt find the Path that leads above; nay, that Image shall become thy Guide itself, because the Sight [Divine] hath this peculiar [charm], it holdeth fast and draweth unto it those who succeed in opening their eyes, just as, they say, the magnet [draweth] iron.

5

THOUGH UNMANIFEST GOD IS MOST MANIFEST

\<This sermon is a fairly straightforward Hermetic version of the "argument by design", a standard approach since ancient times to a proof of the existence of God. Typically, for a Hermetic tractate, its choice of evidence includes a paean on the beauty and perfection of the human form.\>

1. I will recount to thee this sermon (logos) too, O Tat, that thou may'st cease to be without the mysteries of the God beyond all name. And mark thou well how that which to the many seems unmanifest, will grow most manifest for thee.

Now were it manifest, it would not be. For all that is made manifest is subject to becoming, for it hath been made manifest. But the Unmanifest for ever is, for It doth not desire to be made manifest. It ever is, and maketh manifest all other things.

Being Himself unmanifest, as ever being and ever making-manifest, Himself is not made manifest. God is not made Himself; by thinking-manifest \<i.e., thinking into manifestation\>, He thinketh all things manifest.

Now "thinking-manifest" deals with things made alone, for thinking-manifest is nothing else than making.

2. He, then, alone who is not made, 'tis clear, is both beyond all power of thinking-manifest, and is unmanifest.

And as He thinketh all things manifest, He manifests through all things and in all, and most of all in whatsoever things He wills to manifest.

Do thou, then, Tat, my son, pray first unto our Lord and Father, the One-and-Only One, from whom the One doth come, to show His mercy unto thee, in order that thou mayest have the power to catch a thought of this so mighty God, one single beam of Him to shine into thy thinking. For thought alone "sees" the Unmanifest, in that it is itself unmanifest.

If, then, thou hast the power, He will, Tat, manifest to thy mind's eyes. The Lord begrudgeth not Himself to anything, but manifests Himself through the whole world.

Thou hast the power of taking thought, of seeing it and grasping it in thy own "hands", and gazing face to face upon God's Image. But if what is within thee even is unmanifest to thee, how, then, shall He Himself who is within thy self be manifest for thee by means of [outer] eyes?

3. But if thou wouldst "see" him, bethink thee of the sun, bethink thee of moon's course, bethink thee of the order of the stars. Who is the One who watcheth o'er that order? For every order hath its boundaries marked out by place and number.

The sun's the greatest god of gods in heaven; to whom all of the heavenly gods give place as unto king and master. And he, this so-great one, he greater than the earth and sea, endures to have above him circling smaller stars than him. Out of respect to Whom, or out of fear of Whom, my son, [doth he do this]?

Nor like nor equal is the course each of these stars describes in heaven. Who [then] is He who marketh out the manner of their course and its extent?

4. The Bear up there that turneth round itself, and carries round the whole cosmos with it - Who is the owner of this instrument? Who He who hath set round the sea its bounds? Who He who hath set on its seat the earth?

For, Tat, there is someone who is the Maker and the Lord of all these things. It cound not be that number, place and measure could be kept without someone to make them. No order whatsoever could be made by that which lacketh place and lacketh measure; nay, even this is not without a lord, my son. For if the orderless lacks something, in that it is not lord of order's path, it also is beneath a lord - the one who hath not yet ordained it order.

5. Would that it were possible for thee to get thee wings, and soar into the air, and, poised midway 'tween earth and heaven, behold the earth's solidity, the sea's fluidity (the flowings of its streams), the spaciousness of air, fire's swiftness, [and] the coursing of the stars, the swiftness of heaven's circuit round them [all]!

Most blessed sight were it, my son, to see all these beneath one sway - the motionless in motion, and the unmanifest made manifest; whereby is made this order of the cosmos and the cosmos which we see of order.

6. If thou would'st see Him too through things that suffer death, both on the earth and in the deep, think of a man's being fashioned in the womb, my son, and strictly scrutinize the art of

Him who fashions him, and learn who fashioneth this fair and godly image of the Man.

Who [then] is He who traceth out the circles of the eyes; who He who boreth out the nostrils and the ears; who He who openeth [the portal of] the mouth; who He who doth stretch out and tie the nerves; who He who channels out the veins; who He who hardeneth the bones; who He who covereth the flesh with skin; who He who separates the fingers and the joints; who He who widens out a treading for the feet; who He who diggeth out the ducts; who He who spreadeth out the spleen; who he who shapeth heart like to a pyramid; who He who setteth ribs together; who He who wideneth the liver out; who He who maketh lungs like to a sponge; who He who maketh belly stretch so much; who he who doth make prominent the parts most honorable, so that they may be seen, while hiding out of sight those of least honor?

7. Behold how many arts [employed] on one material, how many labors on one single sketch; and all exceeding fair, and all in perfect measure, yet all diversified! Who made them all? What mother, or what sire, save God alone, unmanifest, who hath made all things by His Will?

8. And no one saith a statue or a picture comes to be without a sculptor or [without] a painter; doth [then] such workmanship as this exist without a Worker? What depth of blindness, what deep impiety, what depth of ignorance! See, [then] thou ne'er, son Tat, deprivest works of Worker!

Nay, rather is He greater than all names, so great is He, the Father of them all. For verily He is the Only One, and this is His work, to be a father.

9. So, if thou forcest me somewhat too bold, to speak, His being is conceiving of all things and making [them].

And as without its maker its is impossible that anything should be, so ever is He not unless He ever makes all things, in heaven, in air, in earth, in deep, in all of cosmos, in every part that is and that is not of everything. For there is naught in all the world that is not He.

He is Himself, both things that are and things that are not. The things that are He hath made manifest, He keepeth things that are not in Himself.

10. He is the God beyond all name; He the unmanifest, He the most manifest; He whom the mind [alone] can contemplate, He visible to the eyes [as well]; He is the one of no body, the one of many bodies, nay, rather He of every body.

Naught is there which he is not. For all are He and He is all. And for this cause hath He all names, in that they are one Father's. And for this cause hath He Himself no nome, in that He's Father of [them] all.

Who, then, may sing Thee praise of Thee, or [praise] to Thee?

Whither, again, am I to turn my eyes to sing Thy praise; above, below, within, without?

There is no way, no place [is there] about Thee, nor any other thing of things that are.

All [are] in Thee; all [are] from Thee, O Thou who givest all and takest naught, for Thou hast all and naught is there Thou hast not.

11. And when, O Father, shall I hymn Thee? For none can seize Thy hour or time.

For what, again, shall I sing hymn? For things that Thou hast made, or things Thou hast not? For things Thou hast made manifest, or things Thou hast concealed?

How, further, shall I hymn Thee? As being of myself? As having something of mine own? As being other?

For that Thou art whatever I may be; Thou art whatever I may do; Thou art whatever I may speak.

For Thou art all, and there is nothing else which Thou art not. Thou art all that which doth exist, and Thou art what doth not exist - Mind when Thou thinkest, and Father when Thou makest, and God when Thou dost energize, and Good and Maker of all things.

For that the subtler part of matter is the air, of air the soul, of soul the mind, and of mind God.

6

IN GOD ALONE IS GOOD AND ELSEWHERE NOWHERE

\<This sermon on the nature of the Good, like To Asclepius (CH II), relies heavily on the technical language of classical Greek philosophy - a point which some of Mead's translations tend to obscure. "The Good," in Greek thought, is also the self-caused and self-sufficient, and thus has little in common with later conceptions of "goodness," just as the Latin word virtus and the modern Christian concept of "virtue" are very nearly opposites despite their etymological connection. The word "passion" here also needs to be understood in its older sense, as the opposite of "action" (cf. "active" and "passive").

\<The negative attitude toward humanity and the cosmos which appears in this text contrasts sharply with the more positive assessment found, for example, in the Poemandres (CH I) or in the Asclepius - a reminder that these documents are relics of a diverse and not necessarily consistent school of thought. \>

1. Good, O Asclepius, is in none else save in God alone; nay, rather, Good is God Himself eternally.

If it be so, [Good] must be essence, from every kind of motion and becoming free (though naught is free from It), possessed of stable energy around Itself, never too little, nor too much, an ever-full supply. [Though] one, yet [is It] source of all; for what supplieth all is Good. When I, moreover, say [supplieth] altogether [all], it is for ever Good. But this belongs to no one else save God alone.

For He stands not in need of any thing, so that desiring it He should be bad; nor can a single thing of things that are be lost to him, on losing which He should be pained; for pain is part of bad.

Nor is there aught superior to Him, that He should be subdued by it; nor any peer to Him to do Him wrong, or [so that] He should fall in love on its account; nor aught that gives no ear to Him, whereat He should grow angry; nor wiser aught, for Him to envy.

2. Now as all these are non-existent in His being, what is there left but Good alone?

For just as naught of bad is to be found in such transcendent Being, so too in no one of the rest will Good be found.

For in them are all of the other things <i.e., those things which are not Good> - both in the little and the great, both in each severally and in this living one that's greater than them all and the mightiest [of them] <i.e., the cosmos>.

For things subject to birth abound in passions, birth in itself being passible. But where there's passion, nowhere is there Good; and where is Good, nowhere a single passion. For where is day, nowhere is night; and where is night, day is nowhere.

Wherefore in genesis the Good can never be, but only be in the ingenerate.

But seeing that the sharing in all things hath been bestowed on matter, so doth it share in Good.

In this way is the Cosmos Good; that, in so far as it doth make all things, as far as making goes it's Good, but in all other things it is not Good. For it's both passible and subject unto motion, and maker of things passible.

3. Whereas in man by greater or less of bad is good determined. For what is not too bad down here, is good, and good down here is the least part of bad.

It cannot, therefore, be that good down here should be quite clean of bad, for down here good is fouled with bad; and being fouled, it stays no longer good, and staying not it changes into bad.

In God alone, is, therefore, Good, or rather Good is God Himself.

So then, Asclepius, the name alone of Good is found in men, the thing itself nowhere [in them], for this can never be.

For no material body doth contain It - a thing bound on all sides by bad, by labors, pains, desires and passions, by error and by foolish thoughts.

And greatest ill of all, Asclepius, is that each of these things that have been said above, is thought down here to be the greatest good.

And what is still an even greater ill, is belly-lust, the error that doth lead the band of all the other ills - the thing that makes us turn down here from Good.

4. And I, for my part, give thanks to God, that He hath cast it in my mind about the Gnosis of the Good, that it can never be It should be in the world. For that the world is "fullness" of the bad, but God of Good, and Good of God.

The excellencies of the Beautiful are round the very essence [of the Good]; nay, they do seem too pure, too unalloyed; perchance 'tis they that are themselves Its essences.

For one may dare to say, Asclepius - if essence, sooth, He have - God's essence is the Beautiful; the Beautiful is further also Good.

There is no Good that can be got from objects in the world. For all the things that fall beneath the eye are image-things and pictures as it were; while those that do not meet [the eye are the realities], especially the [essence] of the Beautiful and Good.

Just as the eye cannot see God, so can it not behold the Beautiful and Good. For that they are integral parts of God, wedded to Him alone, inseparate familiars, most beloved, with whom God is Himself in love, or they with God.

5. If thou canst God conceive, thou shalt conceive the Beautiful and Good, transcending Light, made lighter than the Light by God. That Beauty is beyond compare, inimitate that Good, e'en as God is Himself.

As, then, thou dost conceive of God, conceive the Beautiful and Good. For they cannot be joined with aught of other things that live, since they can never be divorced from God.

Seek'st thou for God, thou seekest for the Beautiful. One is the Path that leadeth unto It - Devotion joined with Gnosis.

6. And thus it is that they who do not know and do not tread Devotion's Path, do dare to call man beautiful and good, though

he have ne'er e'en in his visions seen a whit that's Good, but is enveloped with every kind of bad, and thinks the bad is good, and thus doth make unceasing use of it, and even feareth that it should be ta'en from him, so straining every nerve not only to preserve but even to increase it.

Such are the things that men call good and beautiful, Asclepius - things which we cannot flee or hate; for hardest thing of all is that we've need of them and cannot live without them.

7

THE GREATEST ILL AMONG MEN IS IGNORANCE OF GOD

<A good solid diatribe in colorful language. One easily imagines it being delivered at the Hermetic equivalent of a tent revival meeting.>

1. Whither stumble ye, sots, who have sopped up the wine of ignorance and can so far not carry it that ye already even spew it forth?

Stay ye, be sober, gaze upwards with the [true] eyes of the heart! And if ye cannot all, yet ye at least who can!

For that the ill of ignorance doth pour o`er all the earth and overwhelm the soul that's battened down within the body, preventing it from fetching port within Salvation's harbors.

2. Be ye then not carried off by the fierce flood, but using the shore-current <lit., "back-current" or "up-current">, ye who can, make for Salvation's port, and, harboring there, seek ye for one to take you by the hand and lead you unto Gnosis' gates.

Where shines clear Light, of every darkness clean; where not a single soul is drunk, but sober all they gaze with their hearts' eyes on Him who willeth to be seen.

No ear can hear Him, nor can eye see Him, nor tongue speak of Him, but [only] mind and heart.

But first thou must tear off from thee the cloak which thou dost wear - the web of ignorance, the ground of bad, corruption's chain, the carapace of darkness, the living death, sensation's corpse, the tomb thou carriest with thee, the robber in thy house, who through the things he loveth, hateth thee, and through the things he hateth, bears thee malice.

3. Such is the hateful cloak thou wearest - that throttles thee [and holds thee] down to it, in order that thou may'st not gaze above, and having seen the Beauty of the Truth, and Good that dwells therein, detest the bad of it; having found out the plot that it hath schemed against thee, by making void of sense those seeming things which men think senses.

For that it hath with mass of matter blocked them up and crammed them full of loathsome lust, so that thou may'st not hear about the things that thou should'st hear, nor see the things thou should'st see.

8

THAT NO ONE OF EXISTING THINGS DOTH PERISH, BUT MEN IN ERROR SPEAK OF THEIR CHANGES AS DESTRUCTIONS AND AS DEATHS

<The idea of cyclic change central to CH III, "The Sacred Sermon", also takes center stage here. A current of ancient speculation grounded in astrology held that as the planets returned after vast cycles of time to the same positions, so all events on earth would repeat themselves precisely into eternity in the future - and had done so from eternity in the past. The technical term for this recurrence, apocatastasis, is the word Mead translates as "restoration" in the beginning of section 4.

<Mead footnotes this tractate as "obscure" and "faulty" in places, and his translation of the beginning of section 3 is conjectural. >

1. [Hermes:] Concerning Soul and Body, son, we now must speak; in what way Soul is deathless, and whence comes the activity in composing and dissolving Body.

For there's no death for aught of things [that are]; the thought this word conveys, is either void of fact, or [simply] by the knocking off a syllable what is called "death", doth stand for "deathless".

For death is of destruction, and nothing in the Cosmos is destroyed. For if Cosmos is second God, a life <or living creature> that cannot die, it cannot be that any part of this immortal life should die. All things in Cosmos are parts of Cosmos, and most of all is man, the rational animal.

2. For truly first of all, eternal and transcending birth, is God the universals' Maker. Second is he "after His image", Cosmos, brought into being by Him, sustained and fed by Him, made deathless, as by his own Sire, living for aye, as ever free from death.

Now that which ever-liveth, differs from the Eternal; for He hath not been brought to being by another, and even if He have been brought to being, He hath not been brought to being by Himself, but ever is brought into being.

For the Eternal, in that It is eternal, is the all. The Father is Himself eternal of Himself, but Cosmos hath become eternal and immortal by the Father.

3. And of the matter stored beneath it <i.e., beneath the cosmos>, the Father made of it a universal body, and packing it together made it spherical - wrapping it round the life - [a sphere] which is immortal in itself, and that doth make materiality eternal.

But He, the Father, full-filled with His ideas, did sow the lives <or living creatures> into the sphere, and shut them in as in a cave, willing to order forth the life with every kind of living.

So He with deathlessness enclosed the universal body, that matter might not wish to separate itself from body's composition, and so dissolve into its own [original] unorder.

For matter, son, when it was yet incorporate <i.e., not yet formed into bodies>, was in unorder. And it doth still retain down here this [nature of unorder] enveloping the rest of the small lives <or living creatures> - that increase-and-decrease which men call death.

4. It is round earthly lives that this unorder doth exist. For that the bodies of the heavenly ones preserve one order allotted to them by the Father as their rule; and it is by the restoration of each one [of them] this order is preserved indissolute.

The "restoration" of bodies on the earth is thus their composition, whereas their dissolution restores them to those bodies which can never be dissolved, that is to say, which know no death. Privation, thus, of sense is brought about, not loss of bodies.

5. Now the third life - Man, after the image of the Cosmos made, [and] having mind, after the Father's will, beyond all earthly lives - not only doth have feeling with the second God <i.e., the Cosmos>, but also hath conception of the first; for of the one 'tis sensible as of a body, while of the other it conceives as bodiless and the Good Mind.

Tat: Doth then this life not perish?

Hermes: Hush, son! and understand what God, what Cosmos [is], what is a life that cannot die, and what a life subject to dissolution.

Yea, understand the Cosmos is by God and in God; but Man by Cosmos and in Cosmos.

The source and limit and the constitution of all things is God.

9
ON THOUGHT AND SENSE

<This somewhat diffuse essay covers a series of topics, starting with (and to some extent from) the concept that the set of perceptions we call "thoughts" and the set we call "sensory perceptions" are not significantly different from each other. The implications of this idea play a significant role in later Hermetic thought, particularly in the areas of magic and the Art of Memory; in this tractate, though, the issues involved are barely touched, and the argument wanders into moral dualisms and the equally important, but distinct, idea that the Cosmos is itself a divine creative power.

<Section 10, in which understanding is held up as the source and precondition of belief, should probably be seen as part of the same ancient debate on the roles of faith and reason that gave rise to Tertullian's famous credo quia absurdum ("I believe because it is absurd"). >

1. I gave the Perfect Sermon (Logos) yesterday, Asclepius; today I think it right, as sequel thereunto, to go through point by point the Sermon about Sense.

Now sense and thought do seem to differ, in that the former has to do with matter, the latter has to do with substance. But unto me both seem to be at-one and not to differ - in men I mean. In other lives <or living creatures> sense is at-oned with Nature, but in men thought.

Now mind doth differ just as much from thought as God doth from divinity. For that divinity by God doth come to be, and by mind thought, the sister of the word (logos) and instruments of one another. For neither doth the word (logos) find utterance without thought, nor is thought manifested without word.

2. So sense and thought both flow together into man, as though they were entwined with one another. For neither without sensing can one think, nor without thinking sense.

But it is possible [they say] to think a thing apart from sense, as those who fancy sights in dreams. But unto me it seems that both of these activities occur in dream-sight, and sense doth pass out of the sleeping to the waking state.

For man is separated into soul and body, and only when the two sides of his sense agree together, does utterance of its thought conceived by mind take place.

3. For it is mind that doth conceive all thoughts - good thoughts when it receives the seeds from God, their contraries when [it receiveth them] from the daimonials; no part of Cosmos being free of daimon, who stealthily doth creep into the daimon who's illumined by God's light <i.e., the human soul>, and sow in him the seed of its own energy.

And mind conceives the seed thus sown, adultery, murder, parricide, [and] sacrilege, impiety, [and] strangling, casting down precipices, and all such other deeds as are the work of evil daimons.

4. The seeds of God, 'tis true, are few, but vast and fair, and good - virtue and self-control, devotion. Devotion is God-gnosis; and he who knoweth God, being filled with all good things, thinks godly thoughts and not thoughts like the many [think].

For this cause they who Gnostic are, please not the many, nor the many them. They are thought mad and laughed at; they're hated and despised, and sometimes even put to death.

For we did say that bad must needs dwell on earth, where 'tis in its own place. Its place is earth, and not Cosmos, as some will sometimes say with impious tongue.

But he who is a devotee of God, will bear with all - once he has sensed the Gnosis. For such an one all things, e'en though they be for others bad, are for him good; deliberately he doth refer them all unto the Gnosis. And, thing most marvelous, 'tis he alone who maketh bad things good.

5. But I return once more to the Discourse (Logos) on Sense. That sense doth share with thought in man, doth constitute him man. But 'tis not [every] man, as I have said, who benefits by thought; for this man is material, that other one substantial.

For the material man, as I have said, [consorting] with the bad, doth have his seed of thought from daimons; while the substantial men [consorting] with the Good, are saved by God.

Now God is Maker of all things, and in His making, He maketh all [at last] like to Himself; but they, while they're becoming good by exercise of their activity, are unproductive things.

It is the working of the Cosmic Course that maketh their becomings what they are, befouling some of them with bad and others of them making clean with good.

For Cosmos, too, Asclepius, possesseth sense-and-thought peculiar to itself, not like that of man; 'tis not so manifold, but as it were a better and a simpler one.

6. The single sense-and-thought of Cosmos is to make all things, and make them back into itself again, as Organ of the Will of God, so organized that it, receiving all the seeds into itself from God, and keeping them within itself, may make all manifest, and [then] dissolving them, make them all new again; and thus, like a Good Gardener of Life, things that have been dissolved, it taketh to itself, and giveth them renewal once again.

There is no thing to which it gives not life; but taking all unto itself it makes them live, and is at the same time the Place of Life and its Creator.

7. Now bodies matter [-made] are in diversity. Some are of earth, of water some, some are of air, and some of fire.

But they are all composed; some are more [composite], and some are simpler. The heavier ones are more [composed], the lighter less so.

It is the speed of Cosmos' Course that works the manifoldness of the kinds of births. For being a most swift Breath, it doth bestow their qualities on bodies together with the One Pleroma - that of Life.

8. God, then, is Sire of Cosmos; Cosmos, of all in Cosmos. And Cosmos is God's Son; but things in Cosmos are by Cosmos.

And properly hath it been called Cosmos [Order]; for that it orders all with their diversity of birth, with its not leaving aught without its life, with the unweariedness of its activity, the speed of its necessity, the composition of its elements, and order of its creatures.

The same, then, of necessity and propriety should have the name of Order.

The sense-and-thought, then, of all lives doth come into them from without, inbreathed by what contains [them all]; whereas Cosmos receives them once for all together with its coming into being, and keeps them as a gift from God.

9. But God is not, as some suppose, beyond the reach of sense-and-thought. It is through superstition men thus impiously speak.

For all the things that are, Asclepius, all are in God, are brought by God to be, and do depend on Him - both things that act through bodies, and things that through soul-substance make [other things] to move, and things that make things live by means of spirit, and things that take unto themselves the things that are worn out.

And rightly so; nay, I would rather say, He doth not have these things; but I speak forth the truth, He is them all Himself. He doth not get them from without, but gives them out [from Him].

This is God's sense-and-thought, ever to move all things. And never time shall be when e'en a whit of things that are shall cease; and when I say "a whit of things that are", I mean a whit of God. For thigs that are, God hath; nor aught [is there] without Him, nor [is] He without aught.

10. These things should seem to thee, Asclepius, if thou dost understand them, true; but if thou dost not understand, things not to be believed.

To understand is to believe, to not believe is not to understand.

My word (logos) doth go before [thee] to the truth. But mighty is the mind, and when it hath been led by word up to a certain point, it hath the power to come before [thee] to the truth.

And having thought o'er all these things, and found them consonant with those which have already been translated by the reason, it hath [e'en now] believed, and found its rest in that Fair Faith.

To those, then, who by God['s good aid] do understand the things that have been said [by us] above, they're credible; but unto those who understand them not, incredible.

Let so much, then, suffice on thought-and-sense.

10
THE KEY

<*This longer tractate presents itself explicitly as a summary or abridgement of the General Sermons (CH II-IX), and discusses the Hermetic view of knowledge and its role in the lives and afterlives of human beings. The attentive reader will notice certain contradictions between the afterlife-teachings of this and previous tractates.*

<*One of the central concepts of The Key, and of Hermetic thought generally, is the distinction between ordinary discursive knowledge which can be expressed in words (in Greek, episteme, which Mead translates somewhat clumsily as "science") and transcendent, unitive knowledge which cannot be communicated (in Greek, gnosis, which Mead simply and sensibly leaves untranslated). The same distinction can be found in many systems of mystical thought. Unlike most of these, though, the Hermetic teachings place value on both.*

<*Readers without much experience in the jargon of Classical philosophy will want to remember that "hylic" means "material", "passible" means "subject to outside forces or to suffering", and "intelligible" means "belonging to the realm of the Mind", and "motion" includes all kinds of*

change. The special implications of "good" in Greek thought - of self-sufficiency and desirability - should also be kept in mind.

< The delightful irony of the Zen moment early in section 9, when Hermes - in the middle of this very substantial lecture - defines the good and pious man as "he who doth not say much or lend his ear to much" and thus rules out both himself and his audience, seems to have been lost on subsequent commentators. >

1. Hermes: My yesterday's discourse (logos) I did devote to thee, Asclepius, and so 'tis [only] right I should devote toafy's to Tat; and this the more because 'tis the abridgement of the General Sermons (Logoi) which he has had addressed to him.

"God, Father and the Good", then, Tat, hath the same nature, or more exactly, energy.

For nature is a predicate of growth, and used of things that change, both mobile and immobile, that is to say, both human and divine, each one of which He willeth into being.

But energy consists in something else, as we have shown in treating of the rest, both things divine and human things; which thing we ought to have in mind when treating of the Good.

2. God's energy is then His Will; further His essence is to will the being of all things. For what is "God and Father and the Good" but the "to be" of all that are not yet? Nay, subsistence self of everything that is; this, then, is God, this Father, this the Good; to Him is added naught of all the rest.

And though the Cosmos, that is to say the Sun, is also sire himself to them that share in him; yet so far is he not the cause of good unto the lives, he is not even of their living.

So that e'en if he be a sire, he is entirely so by compulsion of the Good's Good-will, apart from which nor being nor becoming could e'er be.

3. Again, the parent is the children's cause, both on the father's and the mother's side, only by sharing in the Good's desire [that doth pour] through the Sun. It is the Good which doeth the creating.

And such a power can be possessed by no one else than Him alone who taketh naught, but wills all things to be; I will not, Tat, say "makes".

For that the maker is defective for long periods (in which he sometimes makes, and sometimes doth not make) both in the quality and in the quantity [of what he makes]; in that he sometimes maketh them so many and such like, and sometimes the reverse.

But "God and Father and the Good" is [cause] for all to be. So are at least these things for those who can see.

4. For It doth will to be, and It is both Itself and most of all by reason of Itself. Indeed, all other things beside are just bacause of It; for the distinctive feature of the Good is "that it should be known". Such is the Good, O Tat.

Tat: Thou hast, O father, filled us so full of this so good and fairest sight, that thereby my mind's eye hath now become for me almost a thing to worship.

For that the vision of the Good doth not, like the sun's beam, firelike blaze on the eyes and make them close; nay, on the contrary, it shineth forth and maketh to increase the seeing of the eye, as far as e'er a man hath the capacity to hold the inflow of the radiance that the mind alone can see.

Not only does it come more swiftly down to us, but it does us no harm, and is instinct with all immortal life.

5. They who are able to drink in a somewhat more than others of this Sight, ofttimes from out the body fall asleep in this fairest Spectacle, as was the case with Uranus and Cronus, our forebears. may this be out lot too, O father mine!

Hermes: Yea, may it be, my son! But as it is, we are not yet strung to the Vision, and not as yet have we the power our mind's eye to unfold and gaze upon the Beauty of the Good - Beauty that naught can e'er corrupt or any comprehend.

For only then wilt thou upon It gaze when thou canst say no word concerning It. For Gnosis of the Good is holy silence and a giving holiday to every sense.

6. For neither can he who perceiveth It, perceive aught else; nor he who gazeth on It, gaze on aught else; nor hear aught else, nor stir his body any way. Staying his body's every sense and every motion he stayeth still.

And shining then all round his mond, It shines through his whole soul, and draws it out of body, transforming all of him to essence.

For it is possible, my son, that a man's soul should be made like to God, e'en while it still is in a body, if it doth contemplate the Beauty of the Good.

7. Tat: Made like to God? What dost thou, father, mean?

Hermes: Of every soul apart are transformations, son.

Tat: What meanest thou? Apart?

Hermes: Didst thou not, in the General Sermons, hear that from one Soul - the All-soul - come all these souls which are made to revovlve in all the cosmos, as though divided off?

Of these souls, then, it is that there are many changes, some to a happier lot and some to [just] the contrary of this.

Thus some that were creeping things change into things that in the water dwell, the souls of water things change to earth-dwellers, those that live on earth change to things with wings, and souls that live in air change to men, while human souls reach the first step of deathlessness changed into daimones.

And so they circle to the choir of the Inerrant Gods; for of the Gods there are two choirs, the one Inerrant, and the other Errant. And this is the most perfect glory of the soul.

8. But if a soul on entering the body of a man persisteth in its vice, it neither tasteth deathlessness nor shareth in the Good; but speeding back again it turns into the path that leads to creeping things. This is the sentence of the vicious soul.

And the soul's vice is ignorance. For that the soul who hath no knowledge of the things that are, or knowledge of their nature, or of Good, is blinded by the body's passions and tossed about.

This wretched soul, not knowing what she is, becomes the slave of bodies of strange form in sorry plight, bearing the body as a load; not as the ruler, but the ruled. This [ignorance] is the soul's vice.

9. But on the other hand the virtue of the soul is Gnosis. For he who knows, he good and pious is, and still while on the earth divine.

Tat: But who is such an one, O father mine?

Hermes: He who doth not say much or lend his ear to much. For he who spendeth time in arguing and hearing arguments, doth shadow-fight. For "God, the Father and the Good", is not to be obtained by speech or hearing.

And yet though this is so, there are in all the beings senses, in that they cannot without senses be.

But Gnosis is far different from sense. For sense is brought about by that which hath the mastery o'er us, while Gnosis is the end <i.e., goal> of science, and science is God's gift.

10. All science is incorporeal, the instrument it uses being the mind, just as the mind employs the body.

Both then come into bodies, [I mean] both things that are cognizable by mond alone and things material. For all things must consist out of antithesis and contrariety; and this can otherwise not be.

Tat: Who then is this material God of whom thou speakest?

Hermes: Cosmos is beautiful, but is not good - for that it is material and freely passible; and though it is the first of all things passible, yet is it in the second rank of being and wanting in itself.

And though it never hath itself its birth in time, but ever is, yet is its being in becoming, becoming for all time the genesis of qualities and quantities; for it is mobile and all material motion's genesis.

11. It is intelligible rest that moves material motion in this way, since Cosmos is a sphere - that is to say, a head. And naught of head above's material, as naught of feet below's intelligible, but all material.

And head itself is moved in a sphere-like way - that is to say, as head should move, is mind.

All then that are united to the "tissue" of this "head" (in which is soul) are in their nature free from death - just as when body hath been made in soul, are things that hath more soul than body.

Whereas those things which are at greater distance from this "tissue" - there, where are things which have a greater share of body than of soul - are by their nature subject unto death.

The whole, however, is a life; so that the universe consists of both the hylic and of the intelligible.

12. Again, the Cosmos is the first of living things, while man is second after it, though first of things subject to death.

Man hath the same ensouling power in him as all the rest of living things; yet is he not only not good, but even evil, for that he's subject unto death.

For though the Cosmos also is not good in that it suffers motion, it is not evil, in that it is not subject to death. But man, in that he's subject both to motion and to death, is evil.

13. Now then the principles of man are this-wise vehicled: mind in the reason (logos), the reason in the soul, soul in the spirit <or, rather, vital spirits>, and spirit in the body.

Spirit pervading [body] by means of veins and arteries and blood, bestows upon the living creature motion, and as it were doth bear it in a way.

For this cause some do think the soul is blood, in that they do mistake its nature, not knowing that [at death] it is iteh spirit that must first withdraw into the soul, whereon the blood congeals and veins and arteries are emptied, and then the living creature <or life> is withdrawn; and this is body's death.

14. Now from one Source all things depend; while Source [dependeth] from the One and Only [One]. Source is, moreover, moved to become Source again; whereas the One standeth perpetually and is not moved.

Three then are they: "God, the Father and the Good", Cosmos and man.

God doth contain Cosmos; Cosmos [containeth] man. Cosmos is e'er God's Son, man as it were Cosmos' child.

15. Not that, however, God ignoreth man; nay, right well doth He know him, and willeth to be known.

This is the sole salvation for a man - God's Gnosis. This is the Way Up to the Mount.

By Him alone the soul becometh good, not whiles is good, whiles evil, but [good] out of necessity.

Tat: What dost thou mean, Thrice-greatest one?

Hermes: Behold an infant's soul, my son, that is not yet cut off, because its body is still small and not as yet come unto its full bulk.

Tat: How?

Hermes: A thing of beauty altogether is [such a soul] to see, not yet befouled by body's passions, still all but hanging from the Cosmic Soul!

But when the body grows in bulk and draweth down the soul into its mass, then doth the soul cut off itself and bring upon itself forgetfulness, and no more shareth in the Beautiful and the Good. And this forgetfulness becometh vice.

16. It is the same for them who go out from the body.

For when the soul withdraws into itself, the spirit doth contract itself within the blood, and the soul within the spirit. And then the mind, stripped of its wrappings, and naturally divine, taking unto itself a fiery body, doth traverse every space, after abandoning the soul unto its judgement and whatever chastisement it hath deserved.

Tat: What dost thou, father, mean by this? The mind is parted from soul and soul from spirit? Whereas thou said'st the soul was the mind's vesture, and the soul's the spirit.

17. Hermes: The hearer, son, should think with him who speaks and breathe with him; nay, he should have a hearing subtler than the voice of him who speaks.

It is, son, in a body made of earth that this arrangement of the vestures comes to pass. For in a body made of earth it is impossible the mind should take its seat itself by its own self in nakedness.

For neither is it possible on the one hand the earthly body should contain so much immortality, nor on the other that so great a virtue should endure a body passible in such close contact with it. It taketh, then, the soul for as it were an envelope.

And soul itself, being too and thing divine, doth use the spirit as its envelope, while spirit doth pervade the living creature.

18. When then the mind doth free itself from the earth-body, it straightway putteth on its proper robe of fire, with which it could not dwell in an earth-body.

For earth doth not bear fire; for it is all set in a blaze even by a small spark. And for this cause is water poured around earth, to be a guard and wall, to keep the blazing of the fire away.

But mind, the swiftest thing of all divine outthinkings, and swifter than all elements, hath for its body fire.

For mind being builder doth use the fire as tool for the construction of all things - the Mind of all [for the construction] of all things, but that of man only for things on earth.

Stript of its fire the mind on earth cannot make things divine, for it is human in its dispensation.

19. The soul in man, however - not every soul, but one that pious is - is a daimonic something and divine.

And such a soul when from the body freed, if it have fought the fight of piety - the fight of piety is to know God and to do wrong to no man - such a soul becomes entirely mind.

Whereas the impious soul remains in its own essence, chastised by its own self, and seeking for an earthly body where to enter, if only it be human.

For that no other body can contain a human soul; nor is it right that any human soul should fall into the body of a thing that doth possess no reason. For that the law of God is this: to guard the human soul from such tremendous outrage.

20. Tat: How father, then, is a man's soul chastised?

Hermes: What greater chastisement of any human soul can there be, son, than lack of piety? What fire has so fierce a flame as lack of piety? What ravenous beast so mauls the body as lack of piety the very soul?

Dost thou not see what hosts of ills the impious soul doth bear?

It shrieks and screams: I burn; I am ablaze; I know not what to cry or do; ah, wretched me, I am devoured by all the ills that compass me about; alack, poor me, I neither see nor hear!

Such are the cries wrung from a soul chastised; not, as the many think, and thou, son, dost suppose, that a [man's] soul, passing from body, is changed into a beast.

Such is a very grave mistake, for that the way a soul doth suffer chastisement is this:

21. When mind becomes a daimon, the law requires that it should take a fiery body to execute the services of God; and entering in the soul most impious it scourgeth it with whips made of its sins.

And then the impious soul, scourged with its sins, is plunged in murders, outrage, blasphemy, in violence of all kinds, and all the other things whereby mankind is wronged.

But on the pious soul the mind doth mount and guide it to the Gnosis' Light. And such a soul doth never tire in songs of praise [to God] and pouring blessing on all men, and doing good in word and deed to all, in imitation of its Sire.

22. Wherefore, my son, thou shouldst give praise to God and pray that thou mayst have thy mind Good Mind. It is, then, to a better state the soul doth pass; it cannot to a worse.

Further there is an intercourse of souls; those of the gods have intercourse with those of men, and those of men with souls of creatures which possess no reason.

The higher, further, have in charge the lower; the gods look after men, men after animals irrational, while God hath charge of all; for He is higher than them all and all are less than He.

Cosmos is subject, then, to God, man to the Cosmos, and irrationals to man. But God is o'er them all, and God contains them all.

God's rays, to use a figure, are His energies; the Cosmos's are natures, the arts and sciences are man's.

The energies act through the Cosmos, thence through the nature-rays of Cosmos upon man; the nature-rays [act] through the elements, man [acteth] through the sciences and arts.

23. This is the dispensation of the universe, depending from the nature of the One, pervading [all things] through the Mind, than which is naught diviner nor of greater energy; and naught a greater means for the at-oning men to gods and gods to men.

He, [Mind,] is the Good Daimon. Blessed the soul that is most filled with Him, and wretched is the soul that's empty of the Mind.

Tat: Father, what dost thou mean, again?

Hermes: Dost think then, son, that every soul hath the Good [Mind]? For 'tis of Him we speak, not of the mind in service of which we were just speaking, the mind sent down for [the soul's] chastisement.

24. For soul without the mind "can neither speak nor act". For oftentimes the mind doth leave the soul, and at that time the soul neither sees nor understands, but is just like a thing that hath no reason. Such is the power of mind.

Yet doth it not endure a sluggish soul, but leaveth such a soul tied to the body and bound tight down by it. Such soul, my son, doth not have Mind; and therefore such an one should not be called a man. For that man is a thing-of-life <or animal> divine;

man is not measured with the rest of lives of things upon the earth, but with the lives above in heaven, who are called gods.

Nay more, if we must boldly speak the truth, the true "man" is e'en higher than the gods, or at the [very] least the gods and men are very whit in power each with the other equal.

25. For no one of the gods in heaven shall come down to the earth, o'er-stepping heaven's limit; whereas man doth mount up to heaven and measure it; he knows what things of it are high, what things are low, and learns precisely all things else besides. And greater thing than all; without e'en quitting earth, he doth ascend above. So vast a sweep doth he possess of ecstasy.

For this cause can a man dare say that man on earth is god subject to death, while god in heaven is man from death immune.

Wherefore the dispensation of all things is brought about by means of there, the twain - Cosmos and Man - but by the One.

II

MIND UNTO HERMES

<This complex text is written as a revelation from the divine Mind - the "Man-Shepherd" of CH I - to Hermes, concerning the nature of God and the universe. Difficult enough in its own right, it has been made rather more so by some of Mead's most opaque prose. I have tried to insert clarifications where these are most needed.

<Some notes on terminology may also be useful. The term Aeon here, as in many of the so-called "Gnostic" writings, refers to the timeless and spaceless realm of ideal being. The word cosmos means both "order" and "beauty" - the same root appears in the word "cosmetic". Additionally, the words genesis and becoming in the translation are the same word in the Greek original.

<Finally, the word "inactive" in square brackets near the beginning of section 13 is Mead's, intended to fill a lacuna in the text. The more usual conjecture, as he comments, is "apart from God". >

1. Mind: Master this sermon (logos), then, Thrice-greatest Hermes, and bear in mind the spoken words; and as it hath come unto Me to speak, I will no more delay.

Hermes: As many men say many things, and these diverse, about the All and Good, I have not learned the truth. Make it, then, clear to me, O Master mine! For I can trust the explanation of these things, which comes from Thee alone.

2. Mind: Hear [then], My son, how standeth God and All.

God; Aeon; Cosmos; Time; Becoming.

God maketh Aeon; Aeon, Cosmos; Cosmos, Time; and Time, Becoming <or Genesis>.

The Good - the Beautiful, Wisdom, Blessedness - is <the> essence, as it were, of God; of Aeon, <the essence is> Sameness; of Cosmos, Order; of Time, Change; and of Becoming, Life and Death.

The energies of God are Mind and Soul; of Aeon, lastingness and deathlessness; of Cosmos, restoration and the opposite thereof; of Time, increase and decrease; and of Becoming, quality.

Aeon is, then, in God; Cosmos, in Aeon; in Cosmos; Time; in Time, Becoming.

Aeon stands firm round God; Cosmos is moved in Aeon; Time hath its limits <or is accomplished> in the Cosmos; Becoming doth become in Time.

3. The source, therfore, of all is God; their essence, Aeon; their matter, Cosmos.

God's power is Aeon; Aeon's work is Cosmos - which never hath become, yet ever doth become by Aeon.

Therefore will Cosmos never be destroyed, for Aeon's indestructible; nor doth a whit of things in Cosmos perish, for Cosmos is enwrapped by Aeon round on every side.

Hermes: But God's Wisdom - what is that?

Mind: The Good and Beautiful, and Blessedness, and Virtue's all, and Aeon.

Aeon, then, ordereth [Cosmos], imparting deathlessness and lastingness to matter.

4. For its beginning doth depend on Aeon, as Aeon doth on God.

Now Genesis <or Becoming> and Time, in Heaven and upon the Earth, are of two natures.

In Heaven they are unchangeable and indestructible, but on the Earth they're subject unto change and to destruction.

Further, the Aeon's soul is God; the Cosmos' soul is Aeon; the Earth's soul, Heaven.

And God <is> in Mind; and Mind, in Soul; and Soul, in Matter; and all of them through Aeon.

But all this Body, in which are all the bodies, is full of Soul; and Soul is full of Mind, and Mind of God.

It <i.e., Soul> fills it <i.e., the Body of the Cosmos> from within, and from without encircles it, making the All to live.

Without, this vast and perfect Life [encircles] Cosmos; within, it fills [it with] all lives; above, in Heaven, continuing in sameness; below, on Earth, changing becoming.

5. And Aeon doth preserve this [Cosmos], or by Necessity, or by Foreknowledge, or by Nature, or by whatever else a man supposes or shall suppose. And all is this - God energizing.

The Energy of God is Power that naught can e'er surpass, a Power with which no one can make comparison of any human thing at all, or any thing divine.

Wherefore, O Hermes, never think that aught of things above or things below is like to God, for thou wilt fall from truth. For naught is like to That which hath no like, and is Alone and One.

And do not ever think that any other can possibly possess His power; for what apart from Him is there of life, and deathlessness and change of quality? For what else should He make?

God's not inactive, since all things [then] would lack activity; for all are full of God.

But neither in the Cosmos anywhere, nor in aught else, is there inaction. For that "inaction" is a name that cannot be applied to either what doth make or what is made.

6. But all things must be made; both ever made, and also in accordance with the influence of every space.

For He who makes, is in them all; not stablished in some one of them, nor making one thing only, but making all.

For being Power, He energizeth in the things He makes and is not independent of them - although the things He makes are subject to Him.

Now gaze through Me upon the Cosmos that's now subject to thy sight; regard its Beauty carefully - Body in pure perfection, though one than which there's no more ancient one, ever in prime of life, and ever-young, nay, rather, in even fuller and yet fuller prime!

7. Behold, again, the seven subject Worlds; ordered by Aeon's order, and with their varied course full-filling Aeon!

[See how] all things [are] full of light, and nowhere [is there] fire; for 'tis the love and the blending of the contraries and the dissimilars that doth give birth to light down shining by the energy of God, the Father of all good, the Leader of all order, and Ruler of the seven world-orderings!

[Behold] the Moon, forerunner of them all, the instrument of nature, and the transmuter of its lower matter!

[Look at] the Earth set in the midst of All, foundation of the Cosmos Beautiful, feeder and nurse of things on Earth!

And contemplate the multitude of deathless lives, how great it is, and that of lives subject to death; and midway, between both, immortal [lives] and mortal, [see thou] the circling Moon.

8. And all are full of soul, and all are moved by it, each in its proper way; some round the Heaven, others around the Earth; [see] how the right [move] not unto the left, nor yet the left unto the right; nor the above below, nor the below above.

And that all there are subject unto Genesis, My dearest Hermes, thou hast no longer need to learn of Me. For that they bodies are, have souls, and they are moved.

But 'tis impossible for them to come together into one without some one to bring them [all] together. It must, then, be that such a one as this must be some one who's wholly One.

9. For as the many motions of them [all] are different, and as their bodies are not like, yet has one speed been ordered for

them all, it is impossible that there should be two or more makers for them.

For that one single order is not kept among "the many"; but rivalry will follow of the weaker with the stronger, and they will strive.

And if the maker of the lives that suffer change and death, should be another <from the maker of the immortals>, he would desire to make the deathless ones as well; just as the maker of the deathless ones, [to make the lives] that suffer death.

But come! if there be two - if matter's one, and Soul is one, in whose hands would there be the distribution for the making? Again, if both of them have some of it, in whose hands may be the greater part?

10. But thus conceive it, then; that every living body doth consist of soul and matter, whether [that body be] of an immortal, or a mortal, or an irrational [life].

For that all living bodies are ensouled; whereas, upon the other hand, those that live not, are matter by itself.

And, in like fashion, Soul when in its self is, after its own maker, cause of life; but the cause of all life is He who makes the things that cannot die.

Hermes: How, then, is it that, first, lives subject to death are other than the deathless ones? And, next, how is it that Life which knows no death, and maketh deathlessness, doth not make animals immortal?

11. Mind: First, that there is some one who does these things, is clear; and, next, that He is also One, is very manifest. For, also, Soul is one, and Life is one, and Matter one.

Hermes: But who is He?

Mind: Who may it other be than the One God? Whom else should it beseem to put Soul into lives but God alone? One, then, is God.

It would indeed be most ridiculous, if when thou dost confess the Cosmos to be one, Sun one, Moon one, and Godhead one, thou shouldst wish God Himself to be some one or other of a number!

12. All things, therefore, He makes, in many [ways]. And what great thing is it for God to make life, soul, and deathlessness, and change, when thou [thyself] dost do so many things?

For thou dost see, and speak, and hear, and smell, and taste, and touch, and walk, and think, and breathe. And it is not one man who smells, another one who walks, another one who thinks, and [yet] another one who breathes. But one is he who doth all these.

And yet no one of these could be apart from God. For just as, should thou cease from these, thou wouldst no longer be a living thing, so also, should God cease from them (a thing not law to say), no longer is He God.

13. For if it hath been shown that no thing can [inactive] be, how much less God? For if there's aught he doth not make (if it be law to say), He is imperfect. But if He is not only not inactive, but perfect [God], then He doth make all things.

Give thou thyself to Me, My Hermes, for a little while, and thou shalt understand more easily how that God's work is one, in order that all things may be - that are being made, or once have been, or that are going to be made. And this is, My beloved, Life; this is the Beautiful; this is the Good; this, God.

14. And if thou wouldst in practice understand [this work], behold what taketh place with thee desiring to beget. Yet this is not like unto that, for He doth not enjoy.

For that indeed He hath no other one to share in what He works, for working by Himself, He ever is at work, Himself being what He doth. For did He separate Himself from it, all things would [then] collapse, and all must die, Life ceasing.

But if all things are lives, and also Life is one; then, one is God. And, furthermore, if all are lives, both those in Heaven and those on Earth, and One Life in them all is made to be by God, and God is it <i.e., God is the One Life> - then, all are made by God.

Life is the making-one of Mind and Soul; accordingly Death is not the destruction of those that are at-oned, but the dissolving of their union.

15. Aeon, moreover, is God's image; Cosmos [is] Aeon's; the Sun, of Cosmos; and Man, [the image] of the Sun.

The people call change death, because the body is dissolved, and life, when it's dissolved, withdraws to the unmanifest. But in this sermon (logos), Hermes, My beloved, as thou dost hear, I say the Cosmos also suffers change - for that a part of it each day is made to be in the unmanifest - yet it is ne'er dissolved.

These are the passions of the Cosmos - revolvings and concealments; revolving is conversion and concealment renovation.

16. The Cosmos is all-formed - not having forms external to itself, but changing them itself within itself. Since, then, Cosmos is made to be all-formed, what may its maker be? For that, on the one hand, He should not be void of all form; and, on the other hand, if He's all-formed, He will be like the Cosmos.

Whereas, again, has He a single form, He will thereby be less than Cosmos.

What, then, say we He is? - that we may not bring round our sermon (logos) into doubt; for naught that mind conceives of God is doubtful.

He, then, hath one idea, which is His own alone, which doth not fall beneath the sight, being bodiless, and [yet] by means of bodies manifesteth all [ideas]. And marvel not that there's a bodiless idea.

17. For it is like the form of reason (logos) and mountain-tops in pictures. For they appear to stand out strongly from the rest, but really are quite smooth and flat.

And now consider what is said more boldly, but more truly!

Just as man cannot live apart from Life, so neither can God live without [His] doing good. For this is as it were the life and motion as it were of God - to move all things and make them live.

18. Now some of the things said should bear a sense peculiar to themselves. So understand, for instance, what I'm going to say.

All are in God, [but] not as lying in a place. For place is both a body and immovable, and things that lie do not have motion.

Now things lie one way in the bodiless, another way in being made manifest.

Think, [then,] of Him who doth contain them all; and think, that than the bodiless naught is more comprehensive, or swifter, or more potent, but it is the most comprehensive, the swiftest, and most potent of them all.

19. And, thus, think from thyself, and bid thy soul go unto any land, and there more quickly than thy bidding will it be. And bid it journey oceanwards; and there, again, immediately 'twill be, not as if passing on from place to place, but as if being there.

And bid it also mount to heaven; and it will need no wings, not will aught hinder it, nor fire of sun, nor auther, nor vortex-swirl, nor bodies of the other stars; but, cutting through them all, it will soar up to the last Body [of them all]. And shouldst thou will to break through this as well, and contemplate what is beyond - if there be aught beyond the Cosmos; it is permitted thee.

20. Behold what power, what swiftness, thou dost have! And canst thou do all of these things, and God not [do them]?

Then, in this way know God; as having all things in Himself as thoughts, the whole Cosmos itself.

If, then, thou dost not make thyself like unto God, thou canst not know Him. For like is knowable unto like [alone].

Make, [then,] thyself to grow to the same stature as the Greatness which transcends all measure; leap forth from every body; transcend all time; become Eternity <literally, Aeon>; and [thus] shalt thou know God.

Conceiving nothing is impossible unto thyself, think thyself deathless and able to know all - all arts, all sciences, the way of every life.

Become more lofty than all height, and lower than all depth. Collect into thyself all senses of [all] creatures - of fire, [and] water, dry and moist. Think that thou art at the same time in every place - in earth, in sea, in sky; not yet begotten, in the womb, young, old, [and] dead, in after-death conditions.

And if thou knowest all these things at once - times, places, doings, qualities, and quantities; thou canst know God.

21. But if thou lockest up thy soul within thy body, and dost debase it, saying: I nothing know; I nothing can; I fear the sea; I cannot scale the sky; I know not who I was, who I shall be - what is there [then] between [thy] God and thee?

For thou canst know naught of things beautiful and good so long as thou dost love thy body and art bad.

The greatest bad there is, is not to know God's Good; but to be able to know [Good], and will, and hope, is a Straight Way, the Good's own [Path], both leading there and easy.

If thou but settest thy foot thereon, 'twill meet thee everywhere, 'twill everywhere be seen, both where and when thou dost expect it not - waking, sleeping, sailing, journeying, by night, by day, speaking, [and] saying naught. For there is naught that is not image of the Good.

22. Hermes: Is God unseen?

Mind: Hush! Who is more manifest than He? For this one reason hath He made all things, that through them all thou mayest see Him.

This is the Good of God, this [is] His Virtue - that He may be manifest through all.

For naught's unseen, even of things that are without a body. Mind sees itself in thinking, God in making.

So far these things have been made manifest to thee, Thrice-greatest one! Reflect on all the rest in the same way with thyself, and thou shalt not be led astray.

12
ABOUT THE COMMON MIND

<The "common mind" discussed in this dialogue is the same Mind which appears as a divine power in other parts of the Hermetic literature. It is identical, as well, with the "Good Daimon" whose words are quoted at several points here and elsewhere.

<The Greek word logos - which means both "word" and "reason", among other things - is central to much of the argument, and it's unfortunate that English has no way to express the same complex of meanings. The praise of reason in parts 13-14 is also, and equally, a praise of human language, and this sort of double meaning plays a part elsewhere in this and other parts of the Hermetic literature.>

1. Hermes: The Mind, O Tat, is of God's very essence - (if such a thing as essence of God there be) - and what that is, it and it only knows precisely.

The Mind, then, is not separated off from God's essentiality, but is united to it, as light to sun.

This Mind in men is God, and for this cause some of mankind are gods, and their humanity is nigh unto divinity.

For the Good Daimon said: "Gods are immortal men, and men are mortal gods."

2. But in irrational lives Mind is their nature. For where is Soul, there too is Mind; just as where Life, there is there also Soul.

But in irrational lives their soul is life devoid of mind; for Mind is the in-worker of the souls of men for good - He works on them for their own good.

In lives irrational He doth co-operate with each one's nature; but in the souls of men He counteracteth them.

For every soul, when it becomes embodied, is instantly depraved by pleasure and by pain.

For in a compound body, just like juices, pain and pleasure seethe, and into them the soul, on entering in, is plunged.

3. O'er whatsoever souls the Mind doth, then, preside, to these it showeth its own light, by acting counter to their prepossessions, just as a good physician doth upon the body prepossessed by sickness, pain inflict, burning or lancing it for sake of health.

In just the selfsame way the Mind inflicteth pain on the soul, to rescue it from pleasure, whence comes its every ill.

The great ill of the soul is godlessness; then followeth fancy for all evil things and nothing good.

So, then, Mind counteracting it doth work good on the soul, as the physician health upon the body.

4. But whatsoever human souls have not the Mind as pilot, they share in the same fate as souls of lives irrational.

For [Mind] becomes co-worker with them, giving full play to the desires toward which [such souls] are borne - [desires] that from the rush of lust strain after the irrational; [so that such human souls,] just like irrational animals, cease not irrationally to rage and lust, nor are they ever satiate of ills.

For passions and irrational desires are ills exceeding great; and over these God hath set up the Mind to play the part of judge and executioner.

5. Tat: In that case, father mine, the teaching (logos) as to Fate, which previously thou didst explain to me, risks to be overset.

For that if it be absolutely fated for a man to fornicate, or commit sacrilege, or do some other evil deed, why is he punished - when he hath done the deed from Fate's necessity?

Hermes: All works, my son, are Fate's; and without Fate naught of things corporal - or <i.e., either> good, or ill - can come to pass.

But it is fated, too, that he who doeth ill, shall suffer. And for this cause he doth it - that he may suffer what he suffereth, because he did it.

6. But for the moment, [Tat,] let be the teaching as to vice and Fate, for we have spoken of these things in other [of our sermons]; but now our teaching (logos) is about the Mind: - what Mind can do, and how it is [so] different - in men being such and such, and in irrational lives [so] changed; and [then] again that in irrational lives it is not of a beneficial nature, while that in men it quencheth out the wrathful and the lustful elements.

Of men, again, we must class some as led by reason, and others as unreasoning.

7. But all men are subject to Fate, and genesis and change, for these are the beginning and the end of Fate.

And though all men do suffer fated things, those led by reason (those whom we said Mind doth guide) do not endure <a> like suffering with the rest; but, since they've freed themselves from viciousness, not being bad, they do not suffer bad.

Tat: How meanest thou again, my father? Is not the fornicator bad; the murderer bad; and [so with] all the rest?

Hermes: [I meant not that;] but that the Mind-led man, my son, though not a fornicator, will suffer just as though he had committed fornication, and though he be no murderer, as though he had committed murder.

The quality of change he can no more escape than that of genesis.

But it is possible for one who hath the Mind, to free himself from vice.

8. Wherefore I've ever heard, my son, Good Daimon also say - (and had He set it down in written words, He would have greatly helped the race of men; for He alone, my son, doth truly, as the Firstborn God, gazing on all things, give voice to words (logoi) divine) - yea, once I heard Him say:

"All things are one, and most of all the bodies which the mind alone perceives. Our life is owing to [God's] Energy and Power and Aeon. His Mind is good, so is His Soul as well. And this being so, intelligible things know naught of separation. So, then, Mind, being Ruler of all things, and being Soul of God, can do whate'er it wills."

9. So do thou understand, and carry back this word (logos) unto the question thou didst ask before - I mean about Mind's Fate.

For if thou dost with accuracy, son, eliminate [all] captious arguments (logoi), thou wilt discover that of very truth the Mind, the Soul of God, doth rule o'er all - o'er Fate, and Law, and all things else; and nothing is impossible to it - neither o'er Fate to set a human soul, nor under Fate to set [a soul] neglectful of what comes to pass. Let this so far suffice from the Good Daimon's most good [words].

Tat: Yea, [words] divinely spoken, father mine, truly and helpfully. But further still explain me this.

10. Thou said'st that Mind in lives irrational worked in them as [their] nature, co-working with their impulses.

But impulses of lives irrational, as I do think, are passions.

Now if the Mind co-worketh with [these] impulses, and if the impulses of [lives] irrational be passions, then is Mind also passion, taking its color from the passions.

Hermes: Well put, my son! Thou questionest right nobly, and it is just that I as well should answer [nobly].

11. All things incorporeal when in a body are subject unto passion, and in the proper sense they are [themselves] all passions.

For every thing that moves itself is incorporeal; while every thing that's moved is body.

Incorporeals are further moved by Mind, and movement's <i.e., movement is> passion.

Both, then, are subject unto passion - both mover and the moved, the former being ruler and the latter ruled.

But when a man hath freed himself from body, then is he also freed from passion.

But, more precisely, son, naught is impassible, but all are passible.

Yet passion differeth from possibility; for that the one is active, while the other's passive.

Incorporeals moreover act upon themselves, for either they are motionless or they are moved; but whichsoe'er it be, it's passion.

But bodies are invaribly acted on, and therefore they are passible.

Do not, then, let terms trouble thee; action and passion are both the selfsame thing. To use the fairer sounding term, however, does no harm.

12. Tat: Most clearly hast thou, father mine, set forth the teaching (logos).

Hermes: Consider this as well, my son; that these two things God hath bestowed on man beyond all mortal lives - both mind and speech (logos) equal to immortality. He hath the mind for knowing God and uttered speech (logos) for eulogy of Him.

And if one useth these for what he ought, he'll differ not a whit from the immortals. Nay, rather, on departing from the body, he will be guided by the twain unto the Choir of Gods and Blessed Ones.

13. Tat: Why, father mine! - do not the other lives make use of speech (logos)?

Hermes: Nay, son; but <i.e., only> use of voice; speech is far different from voice. For speech is general among all men, while voice doth differ in each class of living thing.

Tat: But with men also, father mine, according to each race, speech differs.

Hermes: Yea, son, but man is one; so also speech is one and is interpreted, and it is found the same in Egypt, and in Persia, and in Greece.

Thou seemest, son, to be in ignorance of Reason's (Logos) worth and greatness. For that the Blessed God, Good Daimon, hath declared:

"Soul is in Body, Mind in Soul; but Reason (Logos) is in Mind, and Mind in God; and God is Father of [all] these."

14. The Reason, then, is the Mind's image, and Mind God's [image]; while Body is [the image] of the Form; and Form [the image] of the Soul.

The subtlest part of Matter is, then, Air <or vital spirit>; of Air, Soul; of Soul, Mind; and of Mind, God.

And God surroundeth all and permeateth all; while Mind Surroundeth Soul, Soul Air, Air Matter.

Necessity and Providence and Nature are instruments of Cosmos and of Matter's ordering; while of intelligible things each is Essence, and Sameness is their Essence.

But of the bodies of the Cosmos each is many; for through possessiong Sameness, [these] composed bodies, though they do change from one into another of themselves, do natheless keep the incorruption of their Sameness.

15. Whereas in all the rest of composed bodies, of each there is a certain number; for without number structure cannot be, or composition, or decomposition.

Now it is units that give birth to number and increase it, and, being decomposed, are taken back again into themselves.

Matter is one; and this whole Cosmos - the mighty God and image of the mightier One, both with Him unified, and the conserver of the Will and Order of the Father - is filled full of Life.

Naught is there in it throughout the whole of Aeon, the Father's [everlasting] Re-establishment - nor of the whole, nor of the parts - which doth not live.

For not a single thing that's dead, hath been, or is, or shall be in [this] Cosmos.

For that the Father willed it should have Life as long as it should be. Wherefore it needs must be a God.

16. How then, O son, could there be in the God, the image of the Father, in the plenitude of Life - dead things?

For that death is corruption, and corruption destruction.

How then could any part of that which knoweth no corruption be corrupted, or any whit of him the God destroyed?

Tat: Do they not, then, my father, die - the lives in it, that are its parts?

Hermes: Hush, son! - led into error by the term in use for what takes place.

They do not die, my son, but are dissolved as compound bodies.

Now dissolution is not death, but dissolution of a compound; it is dissolved not so that it may be destroyed, but that it may become renewed.

For what is the activity of life? Is it not motion? What then in Cosmos is there that hath no motion? Naught is there, son!

17. Tat: Doth not Earth even, father, seem to thee to have no motion?

Hermes: Nay, son; but rather that she is the only thing which, though in very rapid motion, is also stable.

For how would it not be a thing to laugh at, that the Nurse of all should have no motion, when she engenders and brings forth all things?

For 'tis impossible that without motion one who doth engender, should do so.

That thou should ask if the fourth part <or element> is not inert, is most ridiculous; for the body which doth have no motion, gives sign of nothing but inertia.

18. Know, therefore, generally, my son, that all that is in Cosmos is being moved for increase or for decrease.

Now that which is kept moving, also lives; but there is no necessity that that which lives, should be all same.

For being simultaneous, the Cosmos, as a whole, is not subject to change, my son, but all its parts are subject unto it; yet naught [of it] is subject to corruption, or destroyed.

It is the terms employed that confuse men. For 'tis not genesis that constituteth life, but 'tis sensation; it is not change that constituteth death, but 'tis forgetfulness.

Since, then, these things are so, they are immortal all - Matter, [and] Life, [and] Spirit, Mind [and] Soul, of which whatever liveth, is composed.

19. Whatever then doth live, oweth its immortality unto the Mind, and most of all doth man, he who is both recipient of God, and co-essential with Him.

For with this life alone doth God consort; by visions in the night, by tokens in the day, and by all things doth He foretell the future unto him - by birds, by inward parts, by wind, by tree.

Wherefore doth man lay claim to know things past, things present and to come.

20. Observe this too, my son; that each one of the other lives inhabiteth one portion of the Cosmos - aquatic creatures water, terrene earth, and aery creatures air; while man doth use all these - earth, water air [and] fire; he seeth Heaven, too, and doth contact it with [his] sense.

But God surroundeth all, and permeateth all, for He is energy and power; and it is nothing difficult, my son, to conceive God.

21. But if thou wouldst Him also contemplate, behold the ordering of the Cosmos, and [see] the orderly behavior of its ordering <this is a play on the word "cosmos", which means "order, arrangement">; behold thou the Necessity of things made manifest, and [see] the Providence of things become and things becoming; behold how Matter is all-full of Life; [behold] this so great God in movement, with all the good and noble [ones] - gods, daimones and men!

Tat: But these are purely energies, O father mine!

Hermes: If, then, they're purely energies, my son - by whom, then, are they energized except by God?

Or art thou ignorant, that just as Heaven, Earth, Water, Air, are parts of Cosmos, in just the selfsame way God's parts are Life and Immortality, [and] Energy, and Spirit, and Necessity, and

Providence, and Nature, Soul, and Mind, and the Duration <that is, Aeon or Eternity> of all these that is called Good?

And there are naught of things that have become, or are becoming, in which God is not.

22. Tat: Is He in Matter, father, then?

Hermes: Matter, my son, is separate from God, in order that thou may'st attribute to it the quality of space. But what thing else than mass think'st thou it is, if it's not energized? Whereas if it be energized, by whom is it made so? For energies, we said, are parts of God.

By whom are, then, all lives enlivened? By whom are things immortal made immortal? By whom changed things made changeable?

And whether thou dost speak of Matter, of Body, or of Essence, know that these too are energies of God; and that materiality is Matter's energy, that corporeality is Bodies' energy, and that essentiality doth constituteth the energy of Essence; and this is God - the All.

23. And in the All is naught that is not God. Wherefore nor <i.e., neither> size, nor space, nor quality, nor form, nor time, surroundeth God; for He is All, and All surroundeth all, and permeateth all.

Unto this Reason (Logos), son, thy adoration and thy worship pay. There is one way alone to worship God; [it is] not to be bad.

13

THE SECRET SERMON ON THE MOUNTAIN

<This dialogue is in many ways the culmination of the whole Corpus, summing up the theory of the Hermetic system at the same time as it provides an intriguing glimpse at the practice. The focus of the dialogue is the experience of Rebirth, which involves the replacement of twelve Tormentors within the self by ten divine Powers, leading to the awakening of knowledge of the self and God.

<The "Secret Hymnody" (sections 17-20) is presented as a litany for worship, to be performed twice each day, at sunrise and sunset. It's interesting to note that while the sunrise worship is performed facing east, the sunset worship is done to the south; Egyptian tradition from Pharaonic times onward saw the west as the direction of death.

<The usual difficulties with the multiple meanings of the Greek word logos appear in the translation, compounded by Mead's awkward style. Additionally, one of Mead's few evasions can be found in section 12, where he relates the twelve Tormentors to the "twelve types-of-life". This should more simply, and more accurately, have been translated as "the

twelve signs of the Zodiac". The Theosophical distaste for astrology may well have been involved here. >

1. Tat: [Now] in the General Sermons, father, thou didst speak in riddles most unclear, conversing on Divinity; and when thou saidst no man could e'er be saved before Rebirth, thy meaning thou didst hide.

Further, when I became thy Suppliant, in Wending up the Mount, after thou hadst conversed with me, and when I longed to learn the Sermon (Logos) on Rebirth (for this beyond all other things is just the thing I know not), thou saidst, that thou wouldst give it me - "when thou shalt have become a stranger to the world".

Wherefore I got me ready and made the thought in me a stranger to the world-illusion.

And now do thou fill up the things that fall short in me with what thou saidst would give me the tradition of Rebirth, setting it forth in speech or in the secret way.

I know not, O Thrice-greatest one, from out what matter and what womb Man comes to birth, or of what seed.

2. Hermes: Wisdom that understands in silence [such is the matter and the womb from out which Man is born], and the True Good the seed.

Tat: Who is the sower, father? For I am altogether at a loss.

Hermes: It is the Will of God, my son.

Tat: And of what kind is he that is begotten, father? For I have no share of that essence in me, which doth transcend the senses. The one that is begot will be another one from God, God's Son?

Hermes: All in all, out of all powers composed.

Tat: Thou tellest me a riddle, father, and dost not speak as father unto son.

Hermes: This Race, my son, is never taught; but when He willeth it, its memory is restored by God.

3. Tat: Thou sayest things impossible, O father, things that are forced. Hence answers would I have direct unto these things. Am I a son strange to my father's race?

Keep it not, father, back from me. I am a true-born son; explain to me the manner of Rebirth.

Hermes: What may I say, my son? I can but tell thee this. Whene'er I see within myself the Simple Vision brought to birth out of God's mercy, I have passed through myself into a Body that can never die. And now i am not as I was before; but I am born in Mind.

The way to do this is not taught, and it cannot be seen by the compounded element by means of which thou seest.

Yea, I have had my former composed form dismembered for me. I am no longer touched, but I have touch; I have dimension too; and [yet] am I a stranger to them now.

Thou seest me with eyes, my son; but what I am thou dost not understand [even] with fullest strain of body and of sight.

4. Tat: Into fierce frenzy and mind-fury hast thou plunged me, father, for now no longer do I see myself.

Hermes: I would, my son, that thou hadst e'en passed right through thyself, as they who dream in sleep yet sleepless.

Tat: Tell me this too! Who is the author of Rebirth?

Hermes: The Son of God, the One Man, by God's Will.

5. Tat: Now hast thou brought me, father, unto pure stupefaction. Arrested from the senses which I had before,...<lacuna in original text>; for [now] I see thy Greatness identical with thy distinctive form.

Hermes: Even in this thou art untrue; the mortal form doth change with every day. 'Tis turned by time to growth and waning, as being an untrue thing.

6. Tat: What then is true, Thrice-greatest One?

Hermes: That which is never troubled, son, which cannot be defined; that which no color hath, nor any figure, which is not turned, which hath no garment, which giveth light; that which is comprehensible unto itself [alone], which doth not suffer change; that which no body can contain.

Tat: In very truth I lose my reason, father. Just when I thought to be made wise by thee, I find the senses of this mind of mine blocked up.

Hermes: Thus is it, son: That which is upward borne like fire, yet is borne down like earth, that which is moist like water, yet blows like air, how shalt thou this perceive with sense - the that which is not solid nor yet moist, which naught can bind or loose, of which in power and energy alone can man have any notion - and even then it wants a man who can perceive the Way of Birth in God?

7. Tat: I am incapable of this, O father, then?

Hermes: Nay, God forbid, my son! Withdraw into thyself, and it will come; will, and it comes to pass; throw out of work the body's senses, and thy Divinity shall come to birth; purge from thyself the brutish torments - things of matter.

Tat: I have tormentors then in me, O father?

Hermes: Ay, no few, my son; nay, fearful ones and manifold.

Tat: I do not know them, father.

Hermes: Torment the first is this Not-knowing, son; the second one is Grief; the third, Intemperance; the fourth, Concupiscence; the fifth, Unrighteousness; the sixth is Avarice; the seventh, Error; the eighth is Envy; the ninth, Guile; the tenth is Anger; eleventh, Rashness; the twelfth is Malice.

These are in number twelve; but under them are many more, my son; and creeping through the prison of the body they force the man that's placed therein to suffer in his senses. But they depart (though not all at once) from him who hath been taken pity on by God; and this it is which constitutes the manner of Rebirth. And... <lacuna in the original text> the Reason (Logos).

8. And now, my son, be still and solemn silence keep! Thus shall the mercy that flows on us from God not cease.

Henceforth rejoice, O son, for by the Powers of God thou art being purified for the articulation of the Reason (Logos).

Gnosis of God hath come to us, and when this comes, my son, Not-knowing is cast out.

Gnosis of Joy hath come to us, and on its coming, son, Sorrow will flee away to them who give it room. The Power that follows Joy do I invoke, thy Self-control. O Power most sweet! Let us most gladly bid it welcome, son! How with its coming doth it chase Intemperance away!

9. Now fourth, on Continence I call, the Power against Desire. <lacuna in the original text> This step, my son, is Righteousness' firm seat. For without judgement <other translators read this "without effort"> see how she hath chased Unrighteousness away. We are made righteous, son, by the departure of Unrighteousness.

Power sixth I call to us - that against Avarice, Sharing-with-all.

And now that Avarice is gone, I call on Truth. And Error flees, and Truth is with us.

See how [the measure of] the Good is full, my son, upon Truth's coming. For Envy is gone from us; and unto Truth is joined the Good as well, with Life and Light.

And now no more doth any torment of the Darkness venture nigh, but vanquished [all] have fled with whirring wings.

10. Thou knowest [now], my son, the manner of Rebirth. And when the Ten is come, my son, that driveth out the Twelve, the Birth in understanding <literally "intellectual birth", *noera genesis*> is complete, and by this birth we are made into Gods.

Who then doth by His mercy gain this Birth in God, abandoning the body's senses, knows himself [to be of Light and Life] and that he doth consist of these, and [thus] is filled with bliss.

11. Tat: By God made steadfast, father, no longer with the sight my eyes afford I look on things, but with the energy the Mind doth give me through the Powers.

In Heaven am I, in earth, in water, air; I am in animals, in plants; I'm in the womb, before the womb, after the womb; I'm everywhere!

But further tell me this: How are the torments of the Darkness, when they are twelve in number, driven out by the ten Powers? What is the way of it, Thrice-greatest one?

12. Hermes: This dwelling-place through which we have just passed <i.e., the human body>, my son, is constituted from the circle of the twelve types-of-life, this being composed of elements, twelve in number, but of one nature, an omniform idea. For man's delusion there are disunions in them, son, while in their action they are one. Not only can we never part Rashness from Wrath; they cannot even be distinguished.

According to right reason (logos), then, they <the Twelve> naturally withdraw once and for all, in as much as they are chased out by no less than ten powers, that is, the Ten.

For, son, the Ten is that which giveth birth to souls. And Life and Light are unified there, where the One hath being from the Spirit. According then to reason (logos) the One contains the Ten, the Ten the One.

13. Tat: Father, I see the All, I see myself in Mind.

Hermes: This is, my son, Rebirth - no more to look on things from body's view-point (a thing three ways in space extended)... <lacuna in text>, though this Sermon (Logos) on Rebirth, on which I did not comment - in order that we may not be calumniators of the All unto the multitude, to whom indeed God Himself doth will we should not.

14. Tat: Tell me, O father: This Body which is made up of the Powers, is it at any time dissolved?

Hermes: Hush, [son]! Speak not of things impossible, else wilt thou sin and thy Mind's eye be quenched.

The natural body which our sense perceives is far removed from this essential birth.

The first must be dissolved, the last can never be; the first must die, the last death cannot touch.

Dost thou not know thou hast been born a God, Son of the One, even as I myself?

15. Tat: I would, O father, hear the Praise-giving with hymn which thou didst say thou heardest then when thou wert at the Eight [the Ogdoad] of Powers

Hermes: Just as the Shepherd did foretell [I should], my son, [when I came to] the Eight.

Well dost thou haste to "strike thy tent" <i.e., be free from the physical body>, for thou hast been made pure.

The Shepherd, Mind of all masterhood, hath not passed on to me more than hath been written down, for full well did he know that I should of myself be able to learn all, and hear what I should wish, and see all things.

He left to me the making of fair things; wherefore the Powers within me. e'en as they are in all, break into song.

16. Tat: Father, I wish to hear; I long to know these things.

Hermes: Be still, my son; hear the Praise-giving now that keeps [the soul] in tune, Hymn of Re-birth - a hymn I would not have thought fit so readily to tell, had'st thou not reached the end of all.

Wherefore this is not taught, but is kept hid in silence.

Thus then, my son, stand in a place uncovered to the sky, facing the southern wind, about the sinking of the setting sun, and make thy worship; so in like manner too when he doth rise, with face to the east wind.

Now, son, be still!

The Secret Hymnody

17. Let every nature of the World receive the utterance of my hymn!

Open thou Earth! Let every bolt of the Abyss be drawn for me. Stir not, ye Trees!

I am about to hymn creation's Lord, both All and One.

Ye Heavens open and ye Winds stay still; [and] let God's deathless Sphere receive my word (logos)!

For I will sing the praise of Him who founded all; who fixed the Earth, and hung up Heaven, and gave command that Ocean should afford sweet water [to the Earth], to both those parts that are inhabited and those that are not, for the support and use of every man; who made the Fire to shine for gods and men for every act.

Let us together all give praise to Him, sublime above the Heavens, of every nature Lord!

'Tis He who is the Eye of Mind; may He accept the praise of these my Powers!

18. Ye powers that are within me, hymn the One and All; sing with my Will, Powers all that are within me!

O blessed Gnosis, by thee illumined, hymning through thee the Light that mond alone can see, I joy in Joy of Mind.

Sing with me praises all ye Powers!

Sing praise, my Self-control; sing thou through me, my Righteousness, the praises of the Righteous; sing thou, my Sharing-all, the praises of the All; through me sing, Truth, Truth's praises!

Sing thou, O Good, the Good! O Life and Light, from us to you our praises flow!

Father, I give Thee thanks, to Thee Thou Energy of all my Powers; I give Thee thanks, O God, Thou Power of all my Energies!

19. Thy Reason (Logos) sings through me Thy praises. Take back through me the All into [Thy] Reason - [my] reasonable oblation!

Thus cry the Powers in me. They sing Thy praise, Thou All; they do Thy Will.

From Thee Thy Will; to Thee the All. Receive from all their reasonable oblation. The All that is in us, O Life, preserve; O Light<,> illumine it; O God<,> in-spirit it.

It it Thy Mind that plays the shepherd to Thy Word, O Thou Creator, Bestower of the Spirit [upon all].

20. [For] Thou art God, Thy Man thus cries to Thee through Fire, through Air, through Earth, through Water, [and] through Spirit, through Thy creatures.

'Tis from Thy Aeon I have found praise-giving; and in thy Will, the object of my search, have I found rest.

Tat: By thy good pleasure have I seen this praise-giving being sung, O father; I have set it in my Cosmos too.

Hermes: Say in the Cosmos that thy mind alone can see, my son.

Tat: Yea, father, in the Cosmos that the mind alone can see; for I have been made able by thy Hymn, and by thy Praise-giving my mind hath been illumined. But further I myself as well would from my natural mind send praise-giving to God.

21. Hermes: But not unheedfully, my son.

Tat: Aye. What I behold in mind, that do I say.

To thee, thou Parent of my Bringing into Birth, as unto God I, Tat, send reasonable offerings. o God and Father, thou art the Lord, thou art the Mind. Receive from me oblations reasonable as thou would'st wish; for by thy Will all things have been perfected.

Hermes: Send thou oblation, son, acceptable to God, the Sire of all; but add, my son, too, "through the Word" (Logos).

Tat: I give thee, father, thanks for showing me to sing such hymns.

22. Hermes: Happy am I, my son, that though hast brought the good fruits forth of Truth, products that cannot die.

And now that thou hast learnt this lesson from me, make promise to keep silence on thy virtue, and to no soul, my son, make known the handing on to thee the manner of Rebirth, that we may not be thought to be calumniators.

And now we both of us have given heed sufficiently, both I the speaker and the hearer thou.

In Mind hast thou become a Knower of thyself and our [common] Sire.

THE LIFE AND
TEACHINGS OF THOTH
HERMES TRISMEGISTUS

INTRODUCTION

THUNDER *rolled, lightning flashed, the veil of the Temple was rent from top to bottom. The venerable initiator, in his robes of blue and gold, slowly raised his jeweled wand and pointed with it into the darkness revealed by the tearing of the silken curtain: "Behold the Light of Egypt!" The candidate, in his plain white robe, gazed into the utter blackness framed by the two great Lotus-headed columns between which the veil had hung. As he watched, a luminous haze distributed itself throughout the atmosphere until the air was a mass of shining particles. The face of the neophyte was illumined by the soft glow as he scanned the shimmering cloud for some tangible object. The initiator spoke again: "This Light which ye behold is the secret luminance of the Mysteries. Whence it comes none knoweth, save the 'Master of the Light.' Behold Him!" Suddenly, through the gleaming mist a figure appeared, surrounded by a flickering greenish sheen. The initiator lowered his wand and, bowing his head, placed one hand edgewise against his breast in humble salutation. The neophyte stepped back in awe, partly blinded by the glory of the revealed figure. Gaining courage, the youth gazed again at the Divine One. The Form before him was considerably larger than that of a mortal man. The body seemed partly transparent so that the heart and brain could be seen pulsating and radiant. As the candidate watched, the heart changed into an ibis, and the brain into a flashing emerald. In Its hand this mysterious Being bore a winged rod, entwined with serpents. The aged initiator, raising his wand, cried out in a loud voice: "All hail Thee, Thoth Hermes, Thrice Greatest; all hail Thee, Prince of Men; all hail Thee who standeth upon the head of Typhon!" At the same instant a lurid writhing dragon appeared--a hideous monster, part serpent, part crocodile, and part hog. From its mouth and nostrils poured sheets of flame and horrible sounds echoed through the vaulted chambers. Suddenly Hermes struck the advancing reptile with the serpent-wound staff and with snarling cry the dragon fell over upon its side, while the flames about it slowly died away. Hermes placed His foot upon the skull of the vanquished Typhon. The next instant, with a blaze of unbearable glory that sent the neophyte staggering backward against a pillar, the immortal Hermes, followed by streamers of greenish mist, passed through the chamber and faded into nothingness.*

I
SUPPOSITIONS CONCERNING THE IDENTITY OF HERMES

Iamblichus averred that Hermes was the author of twenty thousand books; Manetho increased the number to more than thirty-six thousand (see James Gardner)--figures which make it evident that a solitary individual, even though he be overshadowed by divine prerogative, could scarcely have accomplished such a monumental labor. Among the arts and sciences which it is affirmed Hermes revealed to mankind were medicine, chemistry, law, arc, astrology, music, rhetoric, Magic, philosophy, geography, mathematics (especially geometry), anatomy, and oratory. Orpheus was similarly acclaimed by the Greeks.

In his *Biographia Antiqua*, Francis Barrett says of Hermes: "* * * if God ever appeared in man, he appeared in him, as is evident both from his books and his Pymander; in which works he has communicated the sum of the Abyss, and the divine knowledge to all posterity; by which he has demonstrated himself to have been not only an inspired divine, but also a deep philosopher, obtaining his wisdom from God and heavenly things, and not from man."

His transcendent learning caused Hermes to be identified with many of the early sages and prophets. In his Ancient Mythology, Bryant writes: "I have mentioned that Cadmus was the same as the Egyptian Thoth; and it is manifest from his being Hermes, and from the invention of letters being attributed to him. " (In the chapter on the theory of *Pythagorean Mathematics* will be found the table of the original Cadmean letters.) Investigators believe that it was Hermes who was known to the Jews as "Enoch," called by Kenealy the "Second Messenger of God." Hermes was accepted into the mythology of the Greeks, later becoming the Mercury of the Latins. He was revered through the form of the planet Mercury because this body is nearest to the sun: Hermes of all creatures was nearest to God, and became known as the Messenger of the Gods.

In the Egyptian drawings of him, Thoth carries a waxen writing tablet and serves as the recorder during the weighing of the souls of the dead in the judgment Hall of Osiris--a ritual of great significance. Hermes is of first importance to Masonic scholars, because he was the author of the Masonic initiatory rituals, which were borrowed from the Mysteries established by Hermes. Nearly all of the Masonic symbols are Hermetic in character. Pythagoras studied mathematics with the Egyptians and from them gained his knowledge of the symbolic geometric solids. Hermes is also revered for his reformation of the calendar system. He increased the year from 360 to 365 days, thus establishing a precedent which still prevails. The appellation "Thrice Greatest" was given to Hermes because he was considered the greatest of all philosophers, the greatest of all priests, and the greatest of all kings. It is worthy of note that the last poem of America's beloved poet, Henry Wadsworth Longfellow, was a lyric ode to Hermes. (See *Chambers' Encyclopædia*.)

2
THE MUTILATED HERMETIC FRAGMENTS

On the subject of the Hermetic books, James Campbell Brown, in his *History of Chemistry*, has written: "Leaving the Chaldean and earliest Egyptian periods, of which we have remains but no record, and from which no names of either chemists or philosophers have come down to us, we now approach the Historic Period, when books were written, not at first upon parchment or paper, but upon papyrus. A series of early Egyptian books is attributed to Hermes Trismegistus, who may have been a real *savant*, or may be a personification of a long succession of writers. * * * He is identified by some with the Greek god Hermes, and the Egyptian Thoth or Tuti, who was the moon-god, and is represented in ancient paintings as ibis-headed with the disc and crescent of the moon. The Egyptians regarded him as the god of wisdom, letters, and the recording of time. It is in consequence of the great respect entertained for Hermes by the old alchemists that chemical writings were called 'hermetic,' and that the phrase 'hermetically sealed' is still in use to designate the closing of a glass vessel by fusion, after the manner of chemical manipulators. We find the same root in the hermetic medicines of Paracelsus, and the hermetic freemasonry of the Middle Ages."

Among the fragmentary writings believed to have come from the stylus of Hermes are two famous works. The first is the *Emerald Table*, and the second is the *Divine Pymander*, or, as it is more commonly called, *The Shepherd of Men*, a discussion of which follows. One outstanding point in connection with Hermes is that he was one of the few philosopher-priests of pagandom upon whom the early Christians did not vent their spleen. Some Church Fathers went so far as to declare that Hermes exhibited many symptoms of intelligence, and that if he had only been born in a more enlightened age so that he might have benefited by *their* instructions he would have been a really great man!

HERMES MERCURIUS TRISMEGISTUS.

THE LIFE AND TEACHINGS OF THOTH HERMES TRISMEGISTUS

In his *Stromata*, Clement of Alexandria, one of the few chroniclers of pagan lore whose writings have been preserved to this age, gives practically all the information that is known concerning the original forty-two books of Hermes and the importance with which these books were regarded by both the temporal and spiritual powers of Egypt. Clement describes one of their ceremonial processions as follows:

"For the Egyptians pursue a philosophy of their own. This is principally shown by their sacred ceremonial. For first advances the Singer, bearing some one of the symbols of music. For they say that he must learn two of the books of Hermes, the one of which contains the hymns of the gods, the second the regulations for the king's life. And after the Singer advances the Astrologer, with a horologe in his hand, and a palm, the symbols of astrology. He must have the astrological books of Hermes, which are four in number, always in his mouth. Of these, one is about the order of the fixed stars that are visible, and another about the conjunctions and luminous appearances of the sun and moon; and the rest respecting their risings. Next in order advances the sacred Scribe, with wings on his head, and in his hand a book and rule, in which were writing ink and the reed, with which they write. And he must be acquainted with what are called hieroglyphics, and know about cosmography and geography, the position of the sun and moon, and about the five planets; also the description of Egypt, and the chart of the Nile; and the description of the equipment of the priests and of the place consecrated to them, and about the measures and the things in use in the sacred rites. Then the Stole-keeper follows those previously mentioned, with the cubit of justice and the cup for libations. He is acquainted with all points called Pædeutic (relating to training) and Moschophaltic (sacrificial). There are also ten books which relate to the honour paid by them to their gods, and containing the Egyptian worship; as that relating to sacrifices, first-fruits, hymns, prayers, processions, festivals, and the like. And behind all walks the Prophet, with the water-vase carried openly in his arms; who is followed by those who carry the issue of loaves. He, as being the governor of the temple, learns the ten books called 'Hieratic'; and they contain all about the laws, and the gods, and the whole of the training of the priests. For the Prophet is, among the Egyptians, also over the distribution of the revenues. There are then forty-two books of Hermes indispensably necessary; of which the six-and-thirty containing the whole philosophy of the Egyptians are learned by the forementioned personages; and the other six, which are medical, by the Pastophoroi (image-bearers),--treating of the structure of the body, and of disease, and instruments, and medicines, and about the eyes, and the last about women.

One of the greatest tragedies of the philosophic world was the loss of nearly all of the forty-two books of Hermes mentioned in the foregoing. These books disappeared during the burning of Alexandria, for the Romans--and later the Christians--realized that until these books were eliminated they could never bring the Egyptians into subjection. The volumes which escaped the fire were buried in the desert and their location is now known to only a few initiates of the secret schools.

THE BOOK OF THOTH

While Hermes still walked the earth with men, he entrusted to his chosen successors the sacred *Book of Thoth*. This work contained the secret processes by which the regeneration of humanity was to be accomplished and also served as the key to his other writings. Nothing definite is known concerning the contents of the *Book of Thoth* other than that its pages were covered with strange hieroglyphic figures and symbols, which gave to those acquainted with their use unlimited power over the spirits of the air and the subterranean divinities. When certain areas of the brain are stimulated by the secret processes of the Mysteries, the consciousness of man is extended and he is permitted to behold the Immortals and enter into the presence of the superior gods. The *Book of Thoth* described the method whereby this stimulation was accomplished. In truth, therefore, it was the "Key to Immortality."

According to legend, the *Book of Thoth* was kept in a golden box in the inner sanctuary of the temple. There was but one key and this was in the possession of the "Master of the Mysteries," the highest initiate of the Hermetic Arcanum. He alone knew what was written in the secret book. The *Book of Thoth* was lost to the ancient world with the decay of the Mysteries, but its faithful initiates carried it sealed in the sacred casket into another land. The book is still in existence and continues to lead the disciples of this age into the presence of the Immortals. No other information can be given to the world concerning it now, but the apostolic succession from the first hierophant initiated by Hermes himself remains unbroken to this day, and those who are peculiarly fitted to serve the Immortals may discover this priceless document if they will search sincerely and tirelessly for it.

It has been asserted that the *Book of Thoth* is, in reality, the mysterious *Tarot* of the Bohemians--a strange emblematic book of seventy-eight leaves which has been in possession of the gypsies since the time when they were driven from their ancient temple, the Serapeum. (According to the Secret Histories the gypsies were originally Egyptian priests.) There are now in the world several secret schools privileged to initiate candidates into the Mysteries, but in nearly every instance they lighted their altar fires from the flaming torch of *Herm*. Hermes in his *Book of Thoth* revealed to all mankind the "One Way," and for ages the wise of every nation and every faith have reached immortality by the "Way" established by Hermes in the midst of the darkness for the redemption of humankind.

❦ 4 ❦
POIMANDRES, THE VISION OF HERMES

The *Divine Pymander of Hermes Mercurius Trismegistus* is one of the earliest of the Hermetic writings now extant. While probably not in its original form, having been remodeled during the first centuries of the Christian Era and incorrectly translated since, this work undoubtedly contains many of the original concepts of the Hermetic cultus. *The Divine Pymander* consists of seventeen fragmentary writings gathered together and put forth as one work. The second book of *The Divine Pymander*, called *Poimandres*, or *The Vision*, is believed to describe the method by which the divine wisdom was first revealed to Hermes. It was after Hermes had received this revelation that he began his ministry, teaching to all who would listen the secrets of the invisible universe as they had been unfolded to him.

The Vision is the most: famous of all the Hermetic fragments, and contains an exposition of Hermetic cosmogony and the secret sciences of the Egyptians regarding the culture and unfoldment of the human soul. For some time it was erroneously called "The Genesis of Enoch," but that mistake has now been rectified. At hand while preparing the following interpretation of the symbolic philosophy concealed within *The Vision of Hermes* the present author has had these reference works: *The Divine Pymander of Hermes Mercurius Trismegistus* (London, 1650), translated out of the Arabic and Greek by Dr. Everard; *Hermetica* (Oxford, 1924), edited by Walter Scott; *Hermes, The Mysteries of Egypt* (Philadelphia, 1925), by Edouard Schure; and the *Thrice-Greatest Hermes* (London, 1906), by G. R. S. Mead. To the material contained in the above volumes he has added commentaries based upon the esoteric philosophy of the ancient Egyptians, together with amplifications derived partly from other Hermetic fragments and partly from the secret arcanum of the Hermetic sciences. For the sake of clarity, the narrative form has been chosen in preference to the original dialogic style, and obsolete words have given place to those in current use.

Hermes, while wandering in a rocky and desolate place, gave himself over to meditation and prayer. Following the secret instructions of the Temple, he gradually freed his higher consciousness from the bondage of his bodily senses; and, thus released, his divine nature revealed to him the mysteries of the transcendental spheres. He beheld a figure, terrible and awe-inspiring. It was the Great Dragon, with wings stretching across the sky and light streaming in all directions from its body. (The Mysteries taught that the Universal Life was personified as a dragon.) The Great Dragon called Hermes by name, and asked him why he thus meditated upon the World Mystery. Terrified by the spectacle, Hermes prostrated himself before the Dragon, beseeching it to reveal its identity. The great creature answered that it was *Poimandres*, the *Mind of the Universe*, the Creative Intelligence, and the Absolute Emperor of all. (Schure identifies Poimandres as the god Osiris.) Hermes then besought Poimandres to disclose the nature of the universe and the constitution of the gods. The Dragon acquiesced, bidding Trismegistus hold its image in his mind.

THOTH, THE IBIS-HEADED.

IMMEDIATELY THE FORM OF POIMANDRES CHANGED. WHERE IT had stood there was a glorious and pulsating Radiance. This Light was the spiritual nature of the Great Dragon itself. Hermes was "raised" into the midst of this Divine Effulgence and the universe of material things faded from his consciousness.

Presently a great darkness descended and, expanding, swallowed up the Light. Everything was troubled. About Hermes swirled a mysterious watery substance which gave forth a smokelike vapor. The air was filled with inarticulate moanings and sighings which seemed to come from the Light swallowed up in the darkness. His mind told Hermes that the Light was the form of the spiritual universe and that the swirling darkness which had engulfed it represented material substance.

Then out of the imprisoned Light a mysterious and Holy Word came forth and took its stand upon the smoking waters. This Word--the Voice of the Light--rose out of the darkness as a great pillar, and the fire and the air followed after it, but the earth and the water remained unmoved below. Thus the waters of Light were divided from the waters of darkness, and from the waters of Light were formed the worlds above and from the waters of darkness were formed the worlds below. The earth and the water next mingled, becoming inseparable, and the Spiritual Word which is called *Reason* moved upon their surface, causing endless turmoil.

Then again was heard the voice of Poimandres, but His form was not revealed: "I Thy God am the Light and the Mind which were before substance was divided from spirit and darkness from Light. And the Word which appeared as a pillar of flame out of the darkness is the Son of God, born of the mystery of the Mind. The name of that Word is *Reason*. Reason is the offspring of Thought and Reason shall divide the Light from the darkness and establish Truth in the midst of the waters. Understand, O Hermes, and meditate deeply upon the mystery. That which in you sees and hears is not of the earth, but is the Word of God incarnate. So it is said that Divine Light dwells in the midst of mortal darkness, and ignorance cannot divide them. The union of the Word and the Mind produces that mystery which is called

Life. As the darkness without you is divided against itself, so the darkness within you is likewise divided. The Light and the fire which rise are the divine man, ascending in the path of the Word, and that which fails to ascend is the mortal man, which may not partake of immortality. Learn deeply of the Mind and its mystery, for therein lies the secret of immortality."

The Dragon again revealed its form to Hermes, and for a long time the two looked steadfastly one upon the other, eye to eye, so that Hermes trembled before the gaze of Poimandres. At the Word of the Dragon the heavens opened and the innumerable Light Powers were revealed, soaring through Cosmos on pinions of streaming fire. Hermes beheld the spirits of the stars, the celestials controlling the universe, and all those Powers which shine with the radiance of the One Fire--the glory of the Sovereign Mind. Hermes realized that the sight which he beheld was revealed to him only because Poimandres had spoken a Word. The Word was Reason, and by the Reason of the Word invisible things were made manifest. Divine Mind--the Dragon--continued its discourse:

"Before the visible universe was formed its mold was cast. This mold was called the *Archetype*, and this Archetype was in the Supreme Mind long before the process of creation began. Beholding the Archetypes, the Supreme Mind became enamored with Its own thought; so, taking the Word as a mighty hammer, It gouged out caverns in primordial space and cast the form of the spheres in the Archetypal mold, at the same time sowing in the newly fashioned bodies the seeds of living things. The darkness below, receiving the hammer of the Word, was fashioned into an orderly universe. The elements separated into strata and each brought forth living creatures. The Supreme Being--the Mind--male and female, brought forth the Word; and the Word, suspended between Light and darkness, was delivered of another Mind called the *Workman*, the *Master-Builder*, or the *Maker of Things*.

"In this manner it was accomplished, O Hermes: The Word moving like a breath through space called forth the *Fire* by the friction of its motion. Therefore, the Fire is called the *Son of Striving*. The Workman passed as a whirlwind through the universe, causing the substances to vibrate and glow with its friction, The Son of Striving thus formed *Seven Governors*, the Spirits of the Planets, whose orbits bounded the world; and the Seven Governors controlled the world by the mysterious power called *Destiny* given them by the Fiery Workman. When the *Second Mind* (The Workman) had organized Chaos, the Word of God rose straightway our of its prison of substance, leaving the elements without Reason, and joined Itself to the nature of the Fiery Workman. Then the Second Mind, together with the risen Word, established Itself in the midst of the universe and whirled the wheels of the Celestial Powers. This shall continue from an infinite beginning to an infinite end, for the beginning and the ending are in the same place and state.

"Then the downward-turned and unreasoning elements brought forth creatures without Reason. Substance could not bestow Reason, for Reason had ascended out of it. The air produced flying things and the waters such as swim. The earth conceived strange four-footed and creeping beasts, dragons, composite demons, and grotesque monsters. Then the Father--the Supreme Mind--being Light and Life, fashioned a glorious Universal Man in Its own image, not an earthy man but a heavenly Man dwelling in the Light of God. The *Supreme Mind* loved the Man It had fashioned and delivered to Him the control of the creations and workmanships.

"The Man, desiring to labor, took up His abode in the sphere of generation and observed the works of His brother--the Second Mind--which sat upon the Ring of the Fire. And having beheld the achievements of the Fiery Workman, He willed also to make things, and His Father gave permission. The Seven Governors, of whose powers He partook, rejoiced and each gave the Man a share of Its own nature.

"The Man longed to pierce the circumference of the circles and understand the mystery of Him who sat upon the Eternal Fire. Having already all power, He stooped down and peeped through the seven Harmonies and, breaking through the strength of the circles, made Himself manifest to Nature stretched out below. The Man, looking into the depths, smiled, for He beheld a shadow upon the earth and a likeness mirrored in the waters, which shadow and likeness were a reflection of Himself. The Man fell in love with His own shadow and desired to descend into it. Coincident with the desire, the Intelligent Thing united Itself with the unreasoning image or shape.

"Nature, beholding the descent, wrapped herself about the Man whom she loved, and the two were mingled. For this reason, earthy man is composite. Within him is the Sky Man, immortal and beautiful; without is Nature, mortal and destructible. Thus, suffering is the result of the Immortal Man's falling in love with His shadow and giving up Reality to dwell in the darkness of illusion; for, being immortal, man has the power of the Seven Governors--also the Life, the Light, and the Word-but being mortal, he is controlled by the Rings of the Governors--Fate or Destiny.

"Of the Immortal Man it should be said that He is hermaphrodite, or male and female, and eternally watchful. He neither slumbers nor sleeps, and is governed by a Father also both male and female, and ever watchful. Such is the mystery kept hidden to this day, for Nature, being mingled in marriage with the Sky Man, brought forth a wonder most wonderful--seven men, all bisexual, male and female, and upright of stature, each one exemplifying the natures of the Seven Governors. These O Hermes, are the seven races, species, and wheels.

"After this manner were the seven men generated. Earth was the female element and water the male element, and from the fire and the æther they received their spirits, and Nature produced bodies after the species and shapes of men. And man received the Life and Light of the Great Dragon, and of the Life was made his Soul and of the Light his Mind. And so, all these composite creatures containing immortality, but partaking of mortality, continued in this state for the duration of a period. They reproduced themselves out of themselves, for each was male and female. But at the end of the period the knot of Destiny was untied by the will of God and the bond of all things was loosened.

"Then all living creatures, including man, which had been hermaphroditical, were separated, the males being set apart by themselves and the females likewise, according to the dictates of Reason.

"Then God spoke to the Holy Word within the soul of all things, saying: 'Increase in increasing and multiply in multitudes, all you, my creatures and workmanships. Let him that is endued with Mind know himself to be immortal and that the cause of death is the love of the body; and let him learn all things that are, for he who has recognized himself enters into the state of Good.'

THE LIFE AND TEACHINGS OF THOTH HERMES TRISMEGISTUS

A GREEK FORM OF HERMES.

"And when God had said this, Providence, with the aid of the Seven Governors and Harmony, brought the sexes together, making the mixtures and establishing the generations, and all things were multiplied according to their kind. He who through the error of attachment loves his body, abides wandering in darkness, sensible and suffering the things of death, but he who realizes that the body is but the tomb of his soul, rises to immortality."

Then Hermes desired to know why men should be deprived of immortality for the sin of ignorance alone. The Great Dragon answered:, To the ignorant the body is supreme and they are incapable of realizing the immortality that is within them. Knowing only the body which is subject to death, they believe in death because they worship that substance which is the cause and reality of death."

Then Hermes asked how the righteous and wise pass to God, to which Poimandres replied: "That which the Word of God said, say I: 'Because the Father of all things consists of Life and Light, whereof man is made.' If, therefore, a man shall learn and understand the nature of Life and Light, then he shall pass into the eternity of Life and Light."

Hermes next inquired about the road by which the wise attained to Life eternal, and Poimandres continued: "Let the man endued with a Mind mark, consider, and learn of himself, and with the power of his Mind divide himself from his not-self and become a servant of Reality."

Hermes asked if all men did not have Minds, and the Great Dragon replied: "Take heed what you say, for I am the Mind--the Eternal Teacher. I am the Father of the *Word*--the Redeemer of all men--and in the nature of the wise the Word takes flesh. By means of the Word, the world is saved. I, *Thought* (Thoth)--the Father of the Word, the Mind--come only unto men that are holy and good, pure and merciful, and that live piously and religiously, and my presence is an inspiration and a help to them, for when I come they immediately know all things and adore the Universal Father. Before such wise and philosophic ones die, they learn to renounce their senses, knowing that these are the enemies of their immortal souls.

"I will not permit the evil senses to control the bodies of those who love me, nor will I allow evil emotions and evil thoughts to enter them. I become as a porter or doorkeeper, and shut out evil, protecting the wise from their own lower nature. But to the wicked, the envious and the covetous, I come not, for such cannot understand the mysteries of *Mind*; therefore, I am unwelcome. I leave them to the avenging demon that they are making in their own souls, for evil each day increases itself and torments man more sharply, and each evil deed adds to the evil deeds that are gone before until finally evil destroys itself. The punishment of desire is the agony of unfulfillment."

Hermes bowed his head in thankfulness to the Great Dragon who had taught him so much, and begged to hear more concerning the ultimate of the human soul. So Poimandres resumed: "At death the material body of man is returned to the elements from which it came, and the invisible divine man ascends to the source from whence he came, namely the *Eighth Sphere*. The evil passes to the dwelling place of the demon, and the senses, feelings, desires, and body passions return to their source, namely the Seven Governors, whose natures in the lower man destroy but in the invisible spiritual man give life.

"After the lower nature has returned to the brutishness, the higher struggles again to regain its spiritual estate. It ascends the seven Rings upon which sit the Seven Governors and returns to each their lower powers in this manner: Upon the first ring sits the Moon, and to it is returned the ability to increase and diminish. Upon the second ring sits Mercury, and to it are returned machinations, deceit, and craftiness. Upon the third ring sits Venus, and to it are returned the lusts and passions. Upon the fourth ring sits the Sun, and to this Lord are returned ambitions. Upon the fifth ring sits Mars, and to it are returned rashness and profane boldness. Upon the sixth ring sits Jupiter, and to it are returned the sense of accumulation and riches. And upon the seventh ring sits Saturn, at the Gate of Chaos, and to it are returned falsehood and evil plotting.

"Then, being naked of all the accumulations of the seven Rings, the soul comes to the Eighth Sphere, namely, the ring of the fixed stars. Here, freed of all illusion, it dwells in the Light and sings praises to the Father in a voice which only the pure of spirit may understand. Behold, O Hermes, there is a great mystery in the Eighth Sphere, for the Milky Way is the seed-ground of souls, and from it they drop into the Rings, and to the Milky Way they return again from the wheels of Saturn. But some cannot climb the seven-runged ladder of the Rings. So they wander in darkness below and are swept into eternity with the illusion of sense and earthiness.

"The path to immortality is hard, and only a few find it. The rest await the Great Day when the wheels of the universe shall be stopped and the immortal sparks shall escape from the sheaths of substance. Woe unto those who wait, for they must return again, unconscious and unknowing, to the seed-ground of stars, and await a new beginning. Those who are saved by the light of the mystery which I have revealed unto you, O Hermes, and which I now bid you to establish among men, shall return again to the Father who dwelleth in the White Light, and shall deliver themselves up to the Light and shall be absorbed into the Light, and in the Light they shall become Powers in God. This is the Way of *Good* and is revealed only to them that have wisdom.

"Blessed art thou, O Son of Light, to whom of all men, I, Poimandres, the Light of the World, have revealed myself. I order you to go forth, to become as a guide to those who wander in darkness, that all men within whom dwells the spirit of *My Mind* (The Universal Mind) may be saved by My Mind in you, which shall call forth My Mind in them. Establish My Mysteries and they shall not fail from the earth, for I am the Mind of the Mysteries and until Mind fails (which is never) my Mysteries cannot fail." With these parting words, Poimandres, radiant with celestial light, vanished, mingling with the powers of the heavens. Raising his eyes unto the heavens, Hermes blessed the

Father of All Things and consecrated his life to the service of the Great Light.

Thus preached Hermes: "O people of the earth, men born and made of the elements, but with the spirit of the Divine Man within you, rise from your sleep of ignorance! Be sober and thoughtful. Realize that your home is not in the earth but in the Light. Why have you delivered yourselves over unto death, having power to partake of immortality? Repent, and *change your minds*. Depart from the dark light and forsake corruption forever. Prepare yourselves to climb through the Seven Rings and to blend your souls with the eternal Light."

Some who heard mocked and scoffed and went their way, delivering themselves to the Second Death from which there is no salvation. But others, casting themselves before the feet of Hermes, besought him to teach them the Way of Life. He lifted them gently, receiving no approbation for himself, and staff in hand, went forth teaching and guiding mankind, and showing them how they might be saved. In the worlds of men, Hermes sowed the seeds of wisdom and nourished the seeds with the Immortal Waters. And at last came the evening of his life, and as the brightness of the light of earth was beginning to go down, Hermes commanded his disciples to preserve his doctrines inviolate throughout all ages. The *Vision of Poimandres* he committed to writing that all men desiring immortality might therein find the way.

In concluding his exposition of the *Vision*, Hermes wrote: "The sleep of the body is the sober watchfulness of the Mind and the shutting of my eyes reveals the true Light. My silence is filled with budding life and hope, and is full of good. My words are the blossoms of fruit of the tree of my soul. For this is the faithful account of what I received from my true Mind, that is Poimandres, the Great Dragon, the Lord of the Word, through whom I became inspired by God with the Truth. Since that day my Mind has been ever with me and in my own soul it hath given birth to the Word: the Word is Reason, and Reason hath redeemed me. For which cause, with all my soul and all my strength, I give praise and blessing unto God the Father, the Life and the Light, and the Eternal Good.

"Holy is God, the Father of all things, the One who is before the First Beginning.

"Holy is God, whose will is performed and accomplished by His own Powers which He hath given birth to out of Himself.

"Holy is God, who has determined that He shall be known, and who is known by His own to whom He reveals Himself.

"Holy art Thou, who by Thy Word (Reason) hast established all things.

"Holy art Thou, of whom all Nature is the image.

"Holy art Thou, whom the inferior nature has not formed.

"Holy art Thou, who art stronger than all powers.

"Holy art Thou, who art greater than all excellency.

"Holy art Thou, who art better than all praise.

"Accept these reasonable sacrifices from a pure soul and a heart stretched out unto Thee.

"O Thou Unspeakable, Unutterable, to be praised with silence!

"I beseech Thee to look mercifully upon me, that I may not err from the knowledge of Thee and that I may enlighten those that are in ignorance, my brothers and Thy sons.

"Therefore I believe Thee and bear witness unto Thee, and depart in peace and in trustfulness into Thy Light and Life.

"Blessed art Thou, O Father! The man Thou hast fashioned would be sanctified with Thee as Thou hast given him power to sanctify others with Thy Word and Thy Truth."

The *Vision of Hermes*, like nearly all of the Hermetic writings, is an allegorical exposition of great philosophic and mystic truths, and its hidden meaning may be comprehended only by those who have been

www.ingramcontent.com/pod-product-compliance
Lightning Source LLC
Chambersburg PA
CBHW052134070526
44585CB00017B/1821